Financial Crime
and Knowledge Workers

Financial Crime and Knowledge Workers

An Empirical Study of Defense Lawyers and White-Collar Criminals

Petter Gottschalk

FINANCIAL CRIME AND KNOWLEDGE WORKERS
Copyright © Petter Gottschalk, 2014.

All rights reserved.

First published in 2014 by PALGRAVE MACMILLAN® in the United States—a division of St. Martin's Press LLC, 175 Fifth Avenue, New York, NY 10010.

Where this book is distributed in the UK, Europe, and the rest of the world, this is by Palgrave Macmillan, a division of Macmillan Publishers Limited, registered in England, company number 785998, of Houndmills, Basingstoke, Hampshire RG21 6XS.

Palgrave Macmillan is the global academic imprint of the above companies and has companies and representatives throughout the world.

Palgrave® and Macmillan® are registered trademarks in the United States, the United Kingdom, Europe and other countries.

ISBN: 978-1-137-38911-4

Library of Congress Cataloging-in-Publication Data

Gottschalk, Petter, 1950–
    Financial crime and knowledge workers : an empirical study of defense lawyers and white-collar criminals / Petter Gottschalk.
      pages cm
    Includes bibliographical references and index.
    ISBN 978-1-137-38911-4 (hardback)
      1. Criminal defense lawyers—United States. 2. Commercial criminals—United States. 3. Defense (Criminal procedure)—United States. 4. White collar crimes—United States. 5. Knowledge management—United States. I. Title.
KF299.C7G68 2014
345.73'0268—dc23

                                                                       2013030926

A catalogue record of the book is available from the British Library.

Design by Amnet.

First edition: February 2014

10 9 8 7 6 5 4 3 2 1

Contents

List of Figures	vii
List of Tables	ix
Introduction	1
1 White-Collar Criminals and Crime	7
2 White-Collar Crime Defense Lawyers	41
3 White-Collar Crime Defense Strategies	55
4 Lawyers as Knowledge Workers	77
5 Law Firms as Knowledge Organizations	93
6 Knowledge Management in Law Firms	107
7 Theoretical Perspectives on Defense Lawyers	123
8 Empirical Study of White-Collar Lawyers	135
9 Prosecution in Court	173
Conclusion	181
Literature	183
Index	193

List of Figures

1.1	Main categories and subcategories of financial crime	22
1.2	Potential predictors of jail sentence in white-collar crime cases	36
2.1	Knowledge rivalry between prosecution and defense in court	47
5.1	Value configuration activities in a law firm as value shop	104
7.1	Stages of lawyer involvement in client affairs	132
8.1	Research model to predict lawyer income	152
8.2	Structural equation model to predict lawyer income	155
8.3	Research model to predict lawyer fame	158
8.4	Research model to predict outcome for criminal and lawyer	161
8.5	Statistical results to predict outcome for criminal and lawyer	164
8.6	Attorney and criminal sectors with variables for each sector	165
8.7	Correlations between variables within attorney and crime sectors	166
8.8	Correlations between variables of attorney and crime sectors	168
8.9	Research model for potential predictors of jail sentence	170
8.10	Research model for potential predictors of lawyer income	172
9.1	Knowledge rivalry controlled by judge expertise	177

List of Tables

1.1	Correlation coefficients for crime variables (statistical significance is measured in terms of probability of possible mistake, where mistake is .05 at * and .01 at **)	38
1.2	Regression analysis for research model	38
1.3	Significance of regression equation	39
1.4	Significance of each predictor variable in regression analysis (Constant means starting point of a line for regression equation)	39
7.1	Theories to provide insights into the role of white-collar lawyers	133
8.1	Correlation analysis for white-collar crime lawyers (statistical significance is measured in terms of probability of possible mistake, where mistake is .05 at * and .01 at **)	141
8.2	Regression analysis with jail sentence as dependent variable	143
8.3	Top white-collar crime cases in terms of years in prison	148
8.4	Ranking of lawyers depending on colleagues, fame, cases, and income (For lawyers Keiserud and Schiøtz there were no cases, but if there were, they would be third on the income list; instead Fougner is third on the income list, and the second on the income list of lawyers is not a white-collar defense lawyer)	150
8.5	Correlation analysis for white-collar criminals and their lawyers	153
8.6	Regression analysis to predict lawyer income	155

8.7	Lawyer income estimates	156
8.8	Correlation analysis for white-collar criminals and their lawyers	159
8.9	Regression analysis for white-collar for lawyer fame	160
8.10	Correlation analysis for white-collar criminals and their lawyers	163
8.11	Correlation coefficients for both attorney and crime sector variables	167
8.12	Correlation coefficients for white-collar criminal characteristics	170
8.13	Correlation coefficients for white-collar attorney characteristics (statistical significance is measured in terms of probability of possible mistake, where mistake is .05 at * and .01 at **)	171

Introduction

Baitar et al. (2012) argue that the only responsibility of a lawyer in the Western legal tradition is to maximize the interests of his or her own client without regard to the impact on the client's opponent or on law enforcement. This book addresses an important and understudied topic: the relationship between white-collar offenders and their lawyers.

In his classic 1985 book *Defending White-Collar Crime: A Portrait of Attorneys at Work*, Kenneth Mann wrote about the differences in guilt issues in crime:

> The white-collar crime defense attorney, like his counterpart handling street crime, typically assumes that his client is guilty. Certainly that assumption held in every case I describe in this book. But unlike the street-crime defense attorney—and this is a critical difference—the white-collar defense attorney does not assume that the government has the evidence to convict his client. Instead, he starts with the assumption that, though his client is guilty, he may be able to keep the government from knowing this or from concluding that it has a strong enough case to prove it. Though in the end he may have to advise his client to plead guilty and bargain, he often starts his case with the expectation of avoiding compromise (5).

The guilt assumption as well as the lack of proof assumption leads white-collar attorneys to select defense approaches depending on the situation. They apply a contingent approach to the defense work.

White-collar crime is defined both in terms of the offense and in terms of the offender. The offense is typically financial crime, such as fraud, tax evasion, corruption, and insider trading. The offender is typically a person of respectability and high social status who commits crime in the course of his occupation (Sutherland, 1940, 1949,

1983). Sutherland's 1949 theory of white-collar crime has served as a catalyst for an area of research that continues today (e.g., Alalehto and Larsson, 2009; Benson and Simpson, 2009; Blickle et al., 2006; Goldstraw-White, 2012; Robb, 2006).

When prosecuted in court, white-collar criminals are defended by lawyers. A lawyer is a knowledge worker specializing in the development and application of legal knowledge to solve client problems (Becker et al., 2001). Lawyers represent their clients in legal matters by presenting evidence and legal arguments as well as providing counsel to clients concerning their legal rights and obligations (Galanter and Palay, 1991; Mountain, 2001; Nottage, 1998; Phillips, 2005).

In this book, we study the role of lawyers and their white-collar criminal clients in terms convictions in court. Specifically, we study relationships between the lawyer's prominence and cases, the magnitude of money involved in crime, and jail sentences for convicted criminals. Our empirical study is based on a sample of convicted white-collar criminals and their attorneys from 2009 to 2012.

Research on the roles of lawyers in white-collar crime is important since it provides new insights into a specific area of legal advice linked to corporate and occupational economic crime.

A logical approach to structuring this book was adopted. It starts with introducing what white-collar crime is and devotes a major part of the first chapter to articulating characteristics of white-collar criminals. White-collar criminals commit financial crimes and, when prosecuted for their crime, are defended by lawyers in court.

Since this book refers to lawyers as knowledge workers in the main title, lawyers and knowledge are introduced in the following chapters. In chapter 2, white-collar crime defense lawyers are introduced. In chapter 3, it is extensively explained why defense of white-collar criminals is so different from other defense assignments. It is all about defense strategies, which include substance defense strategy, information control strategy, and symbolic defense strategy.

The counterparts for attorneys in crime cases are the authorities, who decide whether a suspect shall be prosecuted or not. To avoid and prevent a prosecution decision, the defense lawyer will try to convince the police and prosecution that the client has done nothing that justifies court proceedings. It is all about substance defense strategy at an early stage. The strategic issue for the attorney is how to succeed in stopping the state prosecutor from advancing the investigation from suspicion to prosecution in court. While very different from other crime cases, an attorney's active defense work often starts in the initial phases of a police investigation, when there are only rumors of wrongdoing that may or may not be relevant for criminal law.

Defense lawyers in white-collar crime cases tend to take charge over information control at an early stage, which is according to the information control strategy. Instead of being at the receiving end of documents from the police and prosecution, the attorney is in a position where the flow of information can be monitored. Of particular interest to the attorney is crucial information that can harm the client's case. The flow of harmful facts, insights, and knowledge of causes and effects that might become legal evidence for the police is restricted by the lawyer.

The third and final defense strategy discussed in chapter 3 is the symbolic defense strategy. A symbol is an object or phrase that represents or suggests an idea, belief, or action. Symbolic defense is an alternative and a supplement to substance defense. Substance and symbolic defense are different arenas where the white-collar attorney can work actively to try to make the police close the case, to make the court dismiss the case, and to enable reopening a case to enable the client to plead not guilty. The purpose of symbolic defense is to communicate opinions and intentions by means of symbols. Examples of ways to implement symbolic defense strategy can be found in publicly announced complaints about delays in police investigations, poor police work quality, or other issues related to police and prosecution work.

Chapter 4 moves on to present more insights into lawyers as knowledge workers. Characteristics of knowledge are discussed, as well as differences among know-what, know-how, and know-why. Know-why represents the most advanced kinds of knowledge, as causal relationships in terms of causes and effects are understood and adopted by the lawyer.

Most lawyers work in law firms. Therefore, both chapters 5 and 6 present organizational perspectives on knowledge work. Law firms as knowledge organizations are the topic of chapter 5, while knowledge management in law firms is the topic of chapter 6. A law firm is an organization specialized in the application of legal knowledge to client problems. The client may want to prevent a problem or solve a problem. Lawyers apply a variety of knowledge categories to solve client problems. In defending white-collar criminals, knowledge of the law and knowledge of previous court sentences is not sufficient. Knowledge of accounting, business strategy, organizational structure, organizational culture, deviant behaviors, and anecdotes are needed to defend a client successfully in court.

It is difficult to overstate the importance of theory in understanding white-collar crime lawyers and attorney-client relationships. Theory allows researchers and practitioners to understand and predict outcomes on a basis of insights and probabilities. Theory also allows analysts to describe and explain a process or sequence of events. Theory prevents analysts from being bewildered by the complexity of the real world by providing an organizing tool to create a coherent understanding of the real world. In this perspective, there is obviously a need for a separate chapter dealing with theoretical perspectives on defense lawyers. This is done in chapter 7, where a number of theories are presented: agency theory with principal and agent, transaction cost theory of cooperation, neutralization theory about guilt, attribution theory for explanations, conspiracy theory of external causes, resource-based theory for knowledge access, and stages of growth theory for relationship.

An important strength of this book is that it is based on empirical research. However, it should be signposted that this research, although conducted in a Norwegian context, has examples that are global. Chapter 8 presents the empirical sample of 277 convicted white-collar criminals in Norway. They were all sentenced to jail terms. There are a total of 172 lawyers in the sample, which implies that each lawyer defended 1.6 criminals on average. The youngest lawyer was 26 years old, while the oldest lawyer was 83. The average age of lawyers was 51 years, while the average age of criminals was 48. In chapter 8, results from a number of statistical analyses are presented.

A characteristic of most white-collar criminals as well as their defense lawyers is entrepreneurship. While many white-collar criminals are criminal entrepreneurs, many defense lawyers are entrepreneurs in legal matters. Therefore, the concept of entrepreneurship is applied both in the discussion of lawyers and law firms in chapter 5, as well as in the discussion of criminal entrepreneurial characteristics in chapter 8.

An entrepreneur is a person who operates a new enterprise or venture and assumes some accountability for the inherent risk. The modern view of entrepreneurial talent is as a person who takes the risks involved to undertake a business venture. Entrepreneurship is often difficult and tricky, as many new ventures fail. Most commonly, the term "entrepreneur" applies to someone who creates value by offering a product or service in order to obtain certain benefits such as profit.

The role of white-collar defense agents is to act entrepreneurially and engage in damage limitations to author plausible defenses based on their legal experience and knowledge with the intention of extracting their clients from their predicaments. In an entrepreneurial culture, a law firm stimulates creativity and innovation. The notion of the lawyer as an entrepreneur and of the entrepreneurial nature of practicing the law is an emerging one. As part of the execution of knowledge processes, knowledge lawyers can decide for themselves and is free to decide whether and what knowledge they need, what knowledge they want to evaluate, develop, implement, and communicate. This makes legal knowledge an entrepreneurial endeavor.

Finally, this book discusses in chapter 9 the courtroom as an arena for knowledge rivalry, not only between the public prosecutor and the defense lawyer, but also including the judge. A more knowledgeable and experienced judge will limit the freedom of interpretations of facts, laws, and previous verdicts. A generalist of a judge lacking substance knowledge will open up for the white-collar lawyer to plead not guilty for his defendant based on various strategies applied in court.

This book applies the knowledge perspective in resource-based theory, where knowledge is a resource to commit white-collar crime, to detect crime, to defend criminals, and to sentence criminals to prison. Knowledge is the common denominator in discussing different actors in crime cases: criminals, lawyers, prosecutors, and judges. Our main focus is on the knowledge of white-collar crime defense lawyers, where knowledge is a strategic resource applied in substance defense strategy, information control strategy, and symbolic defense strategy.

White-Collar Criminals and Crime

Who are the perpetrators of white-collar crime? According to a survey conducted by auditing firm KPMG (2009), it has become extremely difficult to profile a typical white-collar criminal. They argue that the person can be of any age group, income level, or tenure of employment. However, they found that most fraudsters are from 26 to 40 years of age, earn a substantial annual income, and have been employed for between 2 and 5 years.

The most economically disadvantaged members of society are not the only ones committing crime. Members of the privileged socioeconomic class are also engaged in criminal behavior (Brightman, 2009). The types of crimes these people commit may differ from those of criminals of lower classes. Some examples of crimes committed by members of the upper classes include business executives bribing public officials to get contracts, chief accountants manipulating balance sheets to avoid taxes, and procurement managers approving fake invoices for personal gain.

Criminal behavior that involves financial crime by members of the privileged socioeconomic class is labeled white-collar crime (Benson and Simpson, 2009). It is often argued that women commit fewer white-collar crimes when compared to men (Haantz, 2002; Holtfreter et al., 2010; Huffman et al., 2010). Suggested reasons for possible gender differences in the commission of white-collar crime include risk aversion and lack of opportunity.

Characteristics of White-Collar Criminals

Sutherland's theory of white-collar crime from 1939 postulates that privileged persons commit financial crime by abusing their powers and the trust placed in them. He defined white-collar crime as crime committed by a person of respectability and high social status in the course of his occupation. According to Brightman (2009), Sutherland's theory of white-collar crime was controversial, particularly since many of the academicians in the audience perceived themselves to be members of the upper echelon of American society. Despite his critics, Sutherland's theory of white-collar criminality served as the catalyst for an area of research that continues today. In particular, differential association theory proposes that a person associating with individuals who have deviant or unlawful mores, values, and norms learns criminal behavior. Certain characteristics play a key role in placing individuals in a position to behave unlawfully, including the proposition that criminal behavior is learned through interaction with other criminals in the upper echelon of society, as well as through interactions occurring in small, intimate groups (Hansen, 2009).

Brightman (2009) differs slightly from Sutherland regarding the definition of white-collar crime. While social status may still determine access to wealth and property, Brightman argues that the term "white-collar crime" should be broader in scope and include virtually any nonviolent act committed for financial gain, regardless of one's social status. For example, access to technology, such as personal computers and the Internet, now allows individuals from all social classes to buy and sell stocks or engage in similar activities that were once the bastion of the financial elite. This would imply that lawful online stock trading should be considered a white-collar crime, but that is not in line with Sutherland's definition or with our definition in this book, where other characteristics of white-collar criminals exclude most online stock traders.

In Sutherland's definition of white-collar crime, white-collar criminals are people of respectability and high social status who commit financial crimes by nonphysical means in the course of their occupations. This excludes many crimes of the upper class such as most cases of murder, adultery, and intoxication, since these are not customarily a part of their procedures (Benson and Simpson, 2009). It also excludes lower-class criminals committing financial crimes, as Brightman (2009) points out.

What Sutherland meant by "respectable" and "high social status individuals" is not quite clear, but we may assume he was referring to what in today's business world are managers and executives. They are, for the most part, the individuals with the power and influence that are associated with respectability and high social status.

Part of the standard view of white-collar offenders is that they are mainstream, law-abiding individuals. They are assumed to be irregular offenders, not people who engage in crime on a regular basis. As Benson and Simpson state, "Unlike the run-of-the-mill common street criminal who usually has had repeated contacts with the criminal justice system, white-collar offenders are thought not to have prior criminal records" (2009: 39). According to this view, when typical white-collar criminals appear before their sentencing judges, they can correctly claim to be first-time offenders. They are wealthy, highly educated, and socially connected. They are elite individuals, according to the description and attitudes of white-collar criminals as suggested by Sutherland (1940, 1949, 1983). Because of these factors, very few white-collar criminals are put on trial, and even fewer upper-class criminals are sentenced to imprisonment. This is in contrast to the prosecution and sentencing of financial criminals who are not wealthy, highly educated, or socially connected, such as individuals abusing the welfare system by getting too much money in public support for nonexistent children.

What Podgor (2007) finds most interesting about Sutherland's work is that a scholar needed to proclaim that crimes of the upper socioeconomic class were in fact crimes that should be prosecuted. It is apparent that prior to the coining of the term "white collar crime," wealth and power allowed some people to escape criminal liability. Sutherland stresses the importance of the offender-based perspective, rather than the offense-based perspective, on white-collar crime. Sutherland's offender-based perspective is applied in this book.

In contrast, the offense-based perspective, as suggested by researchers such as Pontell (2005), stresses the importance of the organization as a vehicle for perpetrating crime. In an organizational setting, it is difficult to distinguish between regular business transactions and criminal business transactions. Criminal transactions appear as ordinary business transactions so as not to attract attention or rouse suspicion.

Pickett and Pickett (2002) use the terms "financial crime," "white-collar crime," and "fraud" interchangeably. They define white-collar crime as the use of deception for illegal gain, normally involving breach of trust and some concealment of the true nature of the activities. White-collar crime is often defined as crime against property (Benson and Simpson, 2009; Heath, 2008), involving the unlawful conversion of property belonging to another to one's own personal use and benefit. Financial crime is profit-driven crime to gain access to and control over property that belongs to someone else. Bucy et al. (2008) argue that white-collar crime refers to nonviolent, business-related violations of state and/or federal criminal statues, and they make a distinction between "leaders" and "followers" in white-collar crime.

White-collar crime can be defined in terms of the offense, the offender, or both. If white-collar crime is defined in terms of the offense, it means crime against property for personal or organizational gain, committed by nonphysical means and by concealment or deception (Benson and Simpson, 2009). If white-collar crime is defined in terms of the offender, it means crime committed by upper-class members of society for personal or organizational gain. These individuals are wealthy, highly educated, and socially connected, and they are typically employed by legitimate organizations (Hansen, 2009).

One of the most famous white-collar criminals is Bernhard Ebbers, former chief executive officer of WorldCom, who was convicted in 2005 of several kinds of fraud and other crimes that led to WorldCom's eventual downfall:

> Bernard Ebbers was extremely wealthy by the time WorldCom began to experience difficulties in 2000. Unfortunately for Ebbers (and ultimately for WorldCom shareholders), his desires exceeded his income. Ebbers's purchases included an enormous ranch, timber lands, and a yacht-building company, and his loans totaled over $400 million. To secure these loans, he used millions of shares of WorldCom stock as collateral. Any time the price of WorldCom stock went down he needed more cash or assets to maintain his collateral. At one of WorldCom's financial meetings, Ebbers told his employees that "his 'lifeblood was in the stock of the company' and that if the price fell below approximately $12 per share, he would be wiped out financially by margin calls." Bernard Ebbers could not allow WorldCom's stock price to fall even if it was realistically inevitable that this would eventually occur. As Judge Winter [the trial judge] stated, "The methods used were specifically intended to create a false picture of profitability even for professional analysts that, in Ebbers's case, was motivated by his personal financial circumstances." (Wagner, 2011: 978)

An American study by Collins and Schmidt (1993) concluded that, as compared to other white-collar individuals, two main characteristics of white-collar criminals are irresponsibility and antisocial behavior. This study examined the construct validity of personality scales, a personality-based integrity test, and homogenous bio data scales as reflected in their ability to discriminate between white-collar criminals and other white-collar employees. A bio data scale is a systematic method of scaling life history experiences. The sample included 365 prison inmates incarcerated in 23 federal correctional institutions for white-collar offenses and 344 individuals employed in upper-level positions of authority.

The various measures were administered to prisoners at the prison sites and to employees at their workplaces. Results showed that nonoffenders scored significantly higher on performance than offenders. Individuals with high scores on the performance scale are described as dependable, reliable, responsible, rule abiding, motivated to high performance on the job, and conscientious in their work behavior.

Furthermore, results showed that nonoffenders scored significantly higher on socialization than offenders. Individuals who score high on this scale are predicted to be dependable, honest, conscientious, and rule abiding, and are not inclined to be opportunistic or manipulative.

The third measure was responsibility, which shares some common characteristics with socialization. The responsibility scale measures the degree to which the individual is conscientious, responsible, dependable, and committed to social, civic, or moral values. Persons who score low on this scale often show antisocial behavior, and, in the workplace, higher scores predict responsibility and attention to duty. Results of Collins and Schmidt's 1993 study showed that offenders scored significantly lower on the responsibility scale than nonoffenders.

The fourth and final measure was tolerance, where nonoffenders had a significantly higher score. Persons scoring high on the tolerance scale are tolerant and trusting, whereas low scorers tend to be suspicious and judgmental toward others and do not believe they can depend on others.

The common themes running through these four scales applied by Collins and Schmidt (1994) are conscientiousness and positive attitudes toward responsible and prosocial behaviors and activities, suggesting that the discriminating factor between offenders and nonoffenders might be conscientiousness.

A 2006 study in Germany concluded that, as compared to other white-collar individuals, two main characteristics of white-collar criminals are hedonism and narcissism. The study by Blickle et al. examined the following hypotheses in their research:

Hypothesis 1: The greater the degree of hedonism present in a business person, the greater is the tendency to commit economic offenses.

Hypothesis 2: The more diagnostic features of a narcissistic personality disorder an individual in a high-ranking white-collar position exhibits, the higher is the probability that this person will commit a white-collar crime.

Hypothesis 3: The lower the behavioral self-control of a person in a high-ranking white-collar position in business, the greater is the probability that this person will commit a white-collar crime.

Hypothesis 4: The higher the rating of conscientiousness that a person in a high-ranking white-collar position gives himself, the lower is the probability that this person will commit a white-collar crime.

The first hypothesis is concerned with hedonism. People for whom material things and enjoyment generally possess a high value are called hedonists. Living in a culture in which a high value is placed on material success and individual wealth can serve as one cause of strong hedonism. With this in mind, Hypothesis 1 states that everything else being equal, the greater the degree of hedonism present in a businessperson, the greater tendency to commit economic offenses.

The second hypothesis is concerned with narcissism. The essential features are a pattern of grandiosity, a need for admiration, and a lack of empathy.

The third hypothesis is concerned with self-control. It is argued that criminals lack self-control. Generally, criminals tend to engage in criminal and similar acts, such as school misconduct when younger, substance abuse, physical aggression, wastefulness, absenteeism and tardiness, reckless driving, social problem behavior, job quitting, or promiscuous sex.

The fourth hypothesis is concerned with conscientiousness. This is a concept with attributes like striving for competence, order, fulfillment of duties, achievement, self-discipline, and deliberate action.

Blickle et al. (2006) tested these hypotheses empirically by surveying white-collar criminal prison inmates and managers working at various companies and then compared the results. Their test was a comparison of offenders with nonoffenders. Their results indicate support for Hypothesis 1, 2, and 3.

Hypothesis 4 was not supported. Blickle et al. (2006) discuss the lack of support for the last hypothesis by arguing that some kind conscientiousness might indeed be needed for individuals committing white-collar crime. Therefore, no statistically significant difference was found between offenders and nonoffenders.

Characteristics of White-Collar Crime

White-collar crime is a broad concept that covers all illegal behavior that takes advantage of positions of professional authority and power as well as opportunity structures available within business for personal and corporate gain (Kempa, 2010):

> Crimes such as embezzlement, fraud, and insider trading, on one hand, and market manipulation, profit exaggeration, and product misrepresentation on the other, add up to a massive criminal domain (252).

Collins and Schmidt (1993) apply a definition provided by the US Department of Justice, where they emphasize entrepreneurship:

> Nonviolent crime for financial gain committed by means of deception by persons whose occupational status is entrepreneurial, professional, or semi-professional and utilizing their special occupational skills and opportunities; also, nonviolent crime for financial gain utilizing deception and committed by anyone having special technical and professional knowledge of business and government, irrespective the person's occupation (296).

Blickle et al. (2006) apply the same kind of definition, but emphasize means of deception, because it is a deceitful kind of crime:

> White-collar crime is non-violent crime for financial gain committed by means of deception (221).

The term "white-collar" refers to the characteristics of the occupational position, such as power in the executive position. Therefore, white-collar crime refers to upper-level occupational crime (Collins and Schmidt, 1993).

If white-collar crime is defined in terms of both perspectives of crime and criminal mentioned here, then white-collar crime has the following characteristics:

- White-collar crime is crime against property for personal or organizational gain, which is committed by nonphysical means

and by concealment or deception. It is deceitful, it is intentional, it breaches trust, and it involves losses.
- White-collar criminals are individuals who are wealthy, highly educated, and socially connected, and they are typically employed by and in legitimate organizations. They are persons of respectability and high social status who commit crimes in the course of their occupations.

In this paper, we apply this definition of white-collar crime, where both characteristics of offense and offender identify the crime. Therefore, white-collar crime is only a subset of financial crime in our perspective: White-collar crime is a violation of the law committed by a person holding a position of respect and authority in the community who uses his or her legitimate occupation to commit financial crime (Eicher, 2009).

White-collar crime contains several clear components (Pickett and Pickett, 2002):

- *It is deceitful.* People involved in white-collar crime tend to cheat, lie, conceal, and manipulate the truth.
- *It is intentional.* Fraud does not result from simple error or neglect but involves purposeful attempts to illegally gain an advantage. As such, it induces a course of action that is predetermined in advance by the perpetrator.
- *It breaches trust.* Business is based primarily on trust. Individual relationships and commitments are geared toward the respective responsibilities of all parties involved. Mutual trust is the glue that binds these relationships together, and it is this trust that is breached when someone tries to defraud another person or business.
- *It involves losses.* Financial crime is based on attempting to secure an illegal gain or advantage, and for this to happen there must be a victim. There must also be a degree of loss or disadvantage. These losses may be written off or insured against or simply accepted. White-collar crime nonetheless constitutes a drain on national resources.
- *It may be concealed.* One feature of financial crime is that it may remain hidden indefinitely. Reality and appearance may not necessarily coincide. Therefore, every business transaction, contract, payment, or agreement may be altered or suppressed to give the appearance of regularity. Spreadsheets, statements,

and sets of accounts cannot always be accepted at face value; this is how some frauds continue undetected for years.
- *There may be an appearance of outward respectability.* Fraud may be perpetrated by persons who appear to be respectable and professional members of society: they may even be employed by the victim.

Price waterhouse Coopers (PwC) is a consulting firm conducting biennial global economic crime surveys. The 2007 economic crime study reveals that many things remain the same: globally, economic crime remains a persistent and intractable problem from which US companies are not immune. More than 50 percent of US companies were affected by it in the two years previous to the 2007 study.

Of companies reporting incidents of fraud, the types of fraud experienced, according to PwC (2007), were as follows:

- 75 percent suffered asset misappropriation
- 36 percent suffered accounting fraud
- 23 percent suffered intellectual property infringement
- 14 percent suffered corruption and bribery
- 12 percent suffered money laundering

Schnatterly (2003) argues that white-collar crime can cost a company from 1 to 6 percent of annual sales, yet little is known about the organizational conditions that can reduce this cost. She found that operational governance, including clarity of policies and procedures, formal cross-company communication, and performance-based pay for the board and for more employees, significantly reduces the likelihood of a crime commission.

McKay et al. (2010) examined the psychopathology of the white-collar criminal acting as a corporate leader. They looked at the impact of a leader's behavior on other employees and the organizational culture developed by that leader. They proposed a 12-step process to explain how an organization can move from being a legally operating organization to one in which unethical behavior is ignored and wrongdoing promoted.

There are a number of explanatory approaches to white-collar crime in business from scientific fields such as economics, sociology, psychiatry, and psychology. In economics, the rational-choice approach implies that if the rationally expected utility of the action clearly outweighs the expected disadvantages resulting from the action, thus leaving some net material advantage, then every person will commit the offense in question. One of the many suppositions of this theory is that people generally strive for enjoyment and the fulfillment of wishes for material goods (Blickle et al., 2006).

The sociological theory of white-collar crime postulates that managers who commit economic offenses live in a social setting, or culture, in which a high value is placed on material success and individual wealth. Both economic theory and sociological theory are of the opinion that strong striving for wealth and enjoyment in some way contributes to economic crimes committed by managers (Blickle).

Psychiatrists view the behavior of white-collar criminals in terms of narcissistic fantasies of omnipresence. White-collar criminals display little guilt and identify themselves with the ideal of achieving success at any price. The essential features of such individuals are a pervasive pattern of grandiosity, a need for admiration, and a lack of empathy (Blickle).

Wagner (2011) puts forward that, counterintuitively, one way to help avoid future accounting scandals such as WorldCom would be the legalization of "fraud-inhibiting insider trading." Fraud-inhibiting insider trading is the subcategory of insider trading where: (1) information is present that would have a price-decreasing effect on stock if made public; (2) the traded stock belongs to an individual who will likely suffer financial injury from a subsequent stock price reduction if the trading does not take place; (3) the individual on whose behalf the trading occurs would have the ability to prevent the release of the information or to release distorted information to the public; and (4) the individual in question did not commit any fraudulent activities prior to availing himself of the safe harbor.

Arguing that prohibiting all insiders trading incentivizes corporate fraud, Wagner's 2011 article begins by giving examples from recent cases in which insider trading could have been used to avoid significant harm. His article particularly focuses on the two most prominent arguments raised against insider trading: (1) that it erodes confidence in the market; and (2) that it is similar to theft and should be prosecuted accordingly. Previously unexamined empirical evidence suggests that the confidence argument may be incorrect and does not suffice to justify a prohibition on fraud-inhibiting insider trading. While the property rights rationale is the strongest position against general insider trading, it might be an insufficient basis to outlaw fraud-inhibiting insider trading.

Variety of White-Collar Crime

Miri-Lavassani et al. (2009) found that identity fraud is the fastest growing white-collar crime in many countries, especially in developed countries. In 2008, the number of identity fraud victims increased by 22 percent to 9.9 million victims. More recently, nonexistant identities are being used more extensively in fraud crime.

Bank fraud is a criminal offense of knowingly executing a scheme to defraud a financial institution. For example in China, bank fraud is expected to increase both in complexity and in quantity as criminals keep upgrading their fraud methods and techniques. Owing to the strong penal emphasis of Chinese criminal law, harsh punishment including the death penalty and life imprisonment has been used frequently for corruption and for what is considered serious bank fraud in China. Cheng and Ma (2009) found, however, that the harshness of the law has not resulted in making the struggle against criminals more effective. The uncertain law and inconsistent enforcement practices have made offenders more fatalistic about the matter: they simply hope they will not be the unlucky ones to get caught.

Fraud is generally defined as the procurement of a private asset or means of advantage through deception or through the neglect of care for the interests of an asset required by duty. In particular, fraud includes heterogeneous forms, such as misappropriation, balance manipulation, insolvency, and capital investment fraud (Füss and Hecker, 2008).

Corruption might be defined as the misuse of entrusted authority for personal benefit. Business corruption is defined by the involvement of private companies, and is usually motivated by corporate profits. Søreide (2006) suggests that in contrast to the term "political corruption" or "petty corruption", where we focus on the interests of politicians or civil servants, we usually emphasize the perspective and the interests of the bribers when applying the term business corruption.

The problem of business corruption can be exemplified by a number of scandals. An example is Exxon Mobile in Kazakhstan, where payments were made to Kazakh officials to obtain a share in the Karachaganak oil and gas field. Another example is the Lesotho Dam project, in which eight international construction companies were charged with bribery after they allegedly paid bribes to win contracts for a large dam project. Yet another example is the Titan Corporation's unofficial payments to the president of Benin to get important business advantages (Søreide, 2006).

In his classic work on and critique of the term white-collar crime, Edelhertz (1983) discusses the variety of crime in terms of categories of white-collar crime. It is a broad range of antisocial behavior that can be examined through different lenses. The behavior can be examined in terms of motivations, victims, or the schemes that are employed. Edelhertz suggests four categories. The first is personal or ad hoc crime. The offender here is pursuing some individual objective and usually has no face-to-face relationship with the victim. Examples would be personal income tax violations, fraud against government entitlement programs, and credit card fraud. The motives here are usually simple greed or very serious actual or perceived need. Schemes are facilitated, and prevention or detection is hampered by the fact that the offender is usually part of a sea of anonymous faces dealt with by government and corporate victims.

The second category involves abuses of trust. Criminal or abusive behavior falling in this category usually involves an offender who has been given custody of the assets of another or power to make decisions that bind another. Embezzlements by employees or fiduciaries, accepting bribes or other favors to grant contracts on behalf of one's government or business employer, misuse of an employer's property or information for private profit, and misuse of labor union pension funds are all examples of this category.

The third category involves offenders who commit crimes that contribute to furtherance of organizational operations, but crime is not the main purpose of the organization. Typical examples are antitrust violations, such as cartels in price fixing arrangements and collusive bidding for public contracts, and violation of corruption acts by bribing a contracting officer. This kind of crime is difficult to deal with because it is submerged in a mass of legitimate activities. It is well hidden and extensively rationalized (Edelhertz, 1983).

Edelhertz's final category is white-collar crime as a business or as the central activity of a venture. It is the business of cheating, to get something for nothing. For these swindlers, the provision of goods, services, or property is only an excuse to grasp money that bears no recognizable relationship to what is provided.

White-Collar Personality Traits

The leadership trait perspective is an important intellectual tradition in leadership research. For white-collar criminals, we may find both bright and dark sides of leadership traits, although the dark sides may be the most prominent when financial crime is committed by white-collar criminals.

There has been a wealth of research into white-collar personality characteristics, and among them, Judge et al. (2009) identify five dark personality traits.

Narcissism is a personality trait that is characterized by arrogance, self-absorption, entitlement, and hostility. Narcissists exhibit an unusually high level of self-love, believing that they are uniquely special and entitled to praise and admiration. As a self-regulatory defense mechanism against a grandiose yet shallow self-concept, narcissists tend to view others as inferior to themselves, often acting in insensitive, hostile, and self-enhancing ways. Narcissist leaders are more likely to interpret information with a self-serving bias and make decisions based on how those decisions will reflect on their reputations.

Hubris exists when an individual has excessive pride, has an inflated sense of self-confidence, and makes self-evaluations in terms of talent, ability, and accomplishment that are much more positive than any reasonable objective assessment would otherwise suggest. Leaders who carry an exaggerated sense of self-worth are likely to be defensive against most forms of critical feedback and respond to negative feedback by questioning the competence of the evaluator and the validity of evaluation technique. When subordinates or peers disagree with hubristic leaders, these leaders deny the credibility and value of negative evaluations.

Social dominance represents a preference for hierarchy and stability to achieve control. Dominant individuals prefer to control conversations, put pressure on others, and demand explanations for otherwise normal activities. Dominating individuals tend to be prejudiced, power hungry, and manipulative.

Machiavellianism is a negative term widely used to define a personality trait characterized by cunning, manipulation, and the use of any means necessary to achieve one's political ends. The term is used to characterize unscrupulous politicians of the sort the Italian writer Machiavelli described in his book *The Prince*. These kinds of leaders are concerned with maximizing opportunities to craft their own personal power.

As already mentioned, a study in Germany concluded that two main characteristics of white-collar criminals are hedonism and narcissism, as compared to other white-collar individuals (Blickle et al., 2006). Similarly, Listwan et al. (2010) found that the neurotic personality type among white-collar workers has an increased probability of criminal behavior.

An interesting aspect of criminal personality is how white-collar prisoners perceive audience reaction. Dhami (2007) studied reactions of the judiciary, media, significant others, prison staff, and other inmates toward these criminals and how these offenders perceived their own offending behavior. Interviews with 14 offenders revealed that they perceived the reaction of the judiciary and media as negative (often punitive), but the reaction of significant others, prison staff, and other inmates as positive (often supportive). Offenders neutralized their own criminal behavior. Perceptions of audience reaction were shaped by offenders' expectations of how others would react and by their own conception of crime.

Behavioral self-control theory can be especially relevant for explaining occupational crime. In the general theory of crime, it is hypothesized that the lower the individual's self-control, the greater the likelihood of his or her involvement in criminal behavior when the opportunity arises (Gottfredson and Hirschi, 1990). Low self-control is defined in terms of personal characteristics, such as impulsiveness, the desire to take risks, and self-centeredness (Meneses and Akers, 2011). Gender and high levels of hedonism have also been shown to be predictors of white-collar crime (Blickle et al., 2006; Collins and Schmidt, 1993). Lack of self-control is a feature in narcissism and psychopathy. Accordingly, Ragatz et al., (2012) found that the white-collar criminals scored high on psychopathology and psychopathic traits. Some characteristics of the psychopath may also be favorable in the business domain, for example, self-centeredness (Babiak, 2007). Babiak et al. (2010) showed that psychopathy scores were positively correlated with being a successful communicator. However, no decisive empirical evidence exists linking psychopathy to white-collar criminality (Williams and Paulhus, 2004).

The great majority of theories and approaches to understand occupational white-collar crime are focused on the individual. The individual-level explanations are centered on personal characteristics and personality malfunctions. When it comes to corporate crime, the approaches aimed at understanding causal factors are primarily at the system level.

Institutional theory of moral collapse might explain the extent of corporate crime. Executives in a deteriorating business will tend to expand into both occupational crime and corporate crime to make profits both personally and for the business. This is caused by moral collapse as a consequence of business collapse. The largest corporations can also more easily absorb the negative impact of legal sanctions that some government or regulatory agencies might impose on them. The largest business enterprises might have better lawyers and other resources, so that they can face legal pursuits in more effective and efficient ways. Therefore, laws and regulations tend to have a much less deterrent effect in the case of large business organizations (Dion, 2009). Gross (1978) suggests that the internal structure and setting of organizations are of such a nature as to raise the probability that the attainment of the goals of the organization will subject the organization to the risk of violating societal laws of organizational behavior.

Financial Crime Categories

A number of illegal activities can occur in both the commercial and public sectors. So long as there are weaknesses that can be exploited for gain, companies and other organizations as well as private individuals will be taken advantage of (Pickett and Pickett, 2002). Therefore, we find a great variety of criminal activities that are classified as financial crime. This chapter attempts to develop main categories as well as sub categories of financial crime. The four main categories are labeled corruption, fraud, theft, and manipulation respectively. Within each main category there are a number of subcategories. This chapter is based on exploratory research to stimulate future research in refining and improving the categories suggested here and illustrated in Figure 1.1.

Fraud Crime

Fraud can be defined as an intentional perversion of truth for the purpose of inducing another person in reliance upon that altered truth to part with some valuable thing belonging to him or to surrender a legal right. Fraud is unlawful and intentional making of a misrepresentation that causes actual prejudice or that is potentially prejudicial to another.

Advance fee fraud. Victims are approached by letter, faxes, or e-mail without prior contact. Victims' addresses are obtained from telephone and e-mail directories, business journals, magazines, and newspapers. A typical advance fraud letter describes the need to

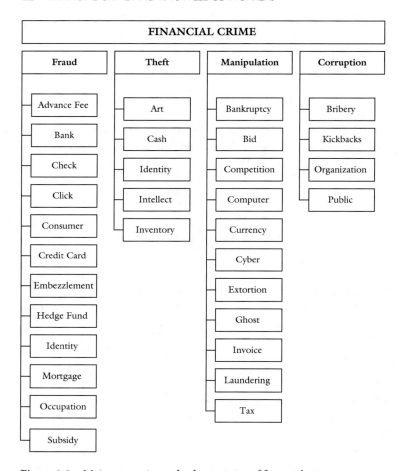

Figure 1.1 Main categories and subcategories of financial crime

move funds out of Nigeria or some other sub-Saharan African country, usually the recovery of contractual funds, crude oil shipments, or inheritance from late kings or governors. This is an external kind of fraud, where advance-fee fraudsters attempt to secure a prepaid commission for an arrangement that is never actually fulfilled or work that is never done.

Bank fraud. Bank fraud is the illegal acquisition of money or other assets owned or held by a financial institution. One US bank fraud case involved Jeffrey Brett Goodin, of Azusa, California, who was sentenced to 70 months imprisonment as a result of his fraudulent activities. Goodin had sent thousands of e-mails to America Online's (AOL) users that appeared to be from AOL's billing department and prompted customers to send personal and credit card information, which he then used to make unauthorized purchases. The e-mails referred the AOL customers to one of several web pages where the victims could in-put their personal and credit information. Goodin controlled these web pages, allowing him to collect the information that enabled him and others to make unauthorized charges on the AOL users' credit or debit cards.

Check fraud. Check fraud refers to a category of criminal acts that involve unlawful use of checks to acquire money or other assets owned by others. When a company check is stolen, altered, or forged, it may be diverted to an unauthorized person who accesses the funds and then closes the account or simply disappears.

Click fraud. When you click on an ad displayed by a search engine, the advertiser typically pays a fee for each click, which is supposed to direct potential buyers to its product. Click fraud occurs when an individual or computer program fraudulently clicks on an online ad without any intention of learning more about the advertiser or making a purchase. It has become a serious problem at Google and other websites that feature pay-per-click online advertising. Some companies hire third parties—typically from low-wage countries—to fraudulently click on a competitor's ads to weaken them by driving up their marketing costs. Click fraud can also be perpetrated with software programs doing the clicking.

Consumer fraud. This kind of fraud constitutes attempts to coerce consumers into paying for goods not received or goods that are substandard, not as specified, or at inflated prices or fees. The growing use of websites as an alternative to unsolicited phone calls or visits to potential customers compounds this problem.

Credit card fraud. This is use of stolen credit card details to secure goods or services in the name of the cardholder. Sometimes a brand new credit card is forged using known details. Cards can be stolen or details obtained from files that are not properly secured. Credit card details may also be purchased from people who are able to access this information. Credit card fraud can be considered a subcategory of identity theft.

Embezzlement is the fraudulent appropriation of property or money entrusted by another to personal use or benefit. The actor first comes into possession of the property with the permission of the owner.

Hedge fund fraud may cause substantial losses for hedge fund investors. "Hedge fund" is defined as a pooled investment that is privately organized and administered by a professional management firm and not widely available to the public. The fund managers often invest a considerable amount of their own wealth in the funds they manage. They tend to refuse to discuss their trading strategies because they do not want competitors to imitate their moves. Hedge fund fraud occurs when the fund manager provides investors with false financial statements claiming large profits, when in fact the money was lost or used to finance the manager's lifestyle.

Identity fraud. Identity fraud occurs when someone abuses the personal information of others to make a profit for themselves, such as opening a credit card account in the victim's name without permission. There are many reported cases where people have had to defend themselves against claims because others have stolen their identity, using personal data such as social security number, address, and date of birth.

Mortgage fraud. To obtain a mortgage for real estate acquisition by a private person, the applicant has to state his or her income. Before the financial crisis in 2008 in the United States, it was determined that 60 percent of the applicants for the loans examined overstated their income by 50 percent or more. Often, borrowers and real estate professionals combined to engage in fraud-for-profit schemes. Such schemes exploited the defining characteristics of subprime lending, such as 100 percent financing and weak underwriting standards. In an industry driven by commissions, lending officers were encouraged to participate in fraud schemes. The more loans the lenders' sales representatives could originate, the more money they made. Mortgage brokers and individuals inside lending institutions thus had powerful incentives to join mortgage fraud schemes by adding dirt to the loan files. They were staging loan files to include false documents as well as ignoring obvious misrepresentations on loan documents.

Occupational fraud. Most developed countries have experienced a number of occupational fraud cases in the last decade, including the Enron, WorldCom, Société Génerale, and the Parmalat frauds in the US, France, and Italy. Occupational fraud is defined as the use of one's occupation for personal enrichment through the deliberate misuse or misapplication of the employing organization's resources or assets. Any fraud committed by an employee, a manager or executive, or by the owner of an organization where the victim is the organization itself may be considered occupational fraud, which is sometimes called internal fraud. Sometimes labeled "financial statement fraud," inaccurate earnings figures may be used as a basis for performance bonuses.

Subsidy crime pertains to criminal offenses committed when government subsidies are granted. A person or a business might provide incorrect information when applying for government subsidies or use the subsidies contrary to intentions and agreements. A similar kind of fraud of the public is sundry frauds, which include illegal price fixing cartels.

Theft Crime

Theft can be defined as the illegal taking of another person's, group's or organization's property without consent.

Art theft is art crime involving theft by burglary, robbery, deception (frauds, fakes, forgery, and false attribution) and might involve money laundering. It has been suggested that the monetary value of stolen works of art is not as great as the value of art frauds, fakes, forgeries, dodgy attributions and bogus provenance in the art, antiques, and antiquities world.

Theft of cash. Theft of cash occurs when someone takes control of money that belongs to someone else. Skimming, one example of theft of cash, occurs when cash is taken before it enters the books. Embezzlement involves direct breach of trust, when someone entrusted with the cash diverts it for personal use. Lapping is a technique whereby the theft of cash or checks is covered up by using later receipts so that the gap in funds is not noticed.

Identity theft. A distinction can be made between identity fraud and identity theft. While identity *fraud* refers to actual misuse of obtained identifiers and engaging in unlawful activities committed by impersonating victims, identity *theft* refers to obtaining those identifiers of an identity holder by being a thief. Identity theft is the crime of acquiring another's personal information without their knowledge and acquiring sufficient data for one individual to successfully impersonate another. It involves securing pieces of an individual's personal information (e.g., birth date, driver's license number, social security number) and using the information extracted from these forms of identification to impersonate the individual.

Intellectual property crime and counterfeiting. Intellectual property crime is abuse of exclusive rights of others as an intangible asset. Intellectual property crime is a serious financial concern for car manufacturers, luxury goods makers, media firms, and drug companies. Counterfeiting is imitating. Counterfeit products are fake replicas of the real product. Most alarmingly is probably that counterfeiting endangers public health, especially in developing countries, where the World Health Organization estimates more than 60 percent of pharmaceuticals are fake goods.

Inventory theft is stealing goods from a company.

Manipulation Crime

Manipulation can be defined as a means of gaining illegal control or influence over others' activities, means, and results to serve one's own purposes.

Bankruptcy crime is criminal acts committed in connection with bankruptcy or liquidation proceedings. A person filing for bankruptcy or a business that has gone into liquidation can hide assets after proceedings have been initiated, thereby preventing creditors from collecting their claims. However, most of the criminal acts associated with bankruptcy crime are typically committed before bankruptcy/liquidation proceedings are initiated, for example, the debtor has failed to keep accounts or has unlawfully withdrawn money from the business.

Bid rigging. When a vendor is given an unfair advantage to defeat an open competition for a given contract, it is known as bid rigging. A vendor may be provided with extra information to bid low but then raise more income through many variations to the set contract. This may be linked to the receipt of kickbacks.

Competition crime is collaborating on and influencing prices, profits and discounts as well as tender and market sharing collaboration. The prohibition regulations in competition laws first of all target cartel collaboration where market participants in a particular industry collaborate in order to limit the competition. They may divide the market between themselves and agree what prices to charge their customers. Prices will be higher than if real competition prevailed in the market.

Computer crime is defined as any violations of criminal law that involve knowledge of computer technology for their perpetration, investigation, or prosecution. This type of crime is an overwhelming problem that has introduced an array of new crime types. The initial role of information and communication technology was to improve the efficiency and effectiveness of organizations. However, the quest for efficiency and effectiveness serves more obscure goals as fraudsters exploit the electronic dimension for personal profits. Examples of computer-related crimes include sabotage, software piracy, and stealing personal data.

Counterfeit currency. The crime of counterfeiting currency is as old as money itself. In the past, nations had used counterfeiting as a means of warfare. The idea was to overflow the enemy's economy with fake banknotes, so that the real value of the said money was reduced, and thereby attacking the economy and general welfare of a society. Currency counterfeiting and money laundering have the potential to destabilize national economies and threaten global security, as these activities are sometimes used by terrorists and other dangerous criminals to finance their activities or conceal their profits.

Cybercrime. Attacks on the cyber security infrastructure of business organizations, cybercrime, can have several goals. One goal pursued by criminals is to gain unauthorized access to the target's sensitive information. Most businesses are vitally dependent on their proprietary information, including new product information, employment records, price lists, and sales figures. An attacker may derive direct economic benefits from gaining access to and/or selling such information or may inflict damage on an organization by impacting upon it. Once access has been attained, attackers can not only extract and use or sell confidential information, they can also modify or delete sensitive information, resulting in significant consequences for their targets.

Extortion is a criminal offense that occurs when a person unlawfully obtains money, property, or services from a person, entity, or institution through coercion. Coercion is the practice of compelling a person or forcing them to behave in an involuntary way. A common abuse of public authority in some countries relates to the enforcement of road traffic regulations or other minor infractions where informal on-the-spot fines—bribes—are negotiated with the alleged offender rather than pursuing a formal prosecution or other legal process. In extreme circumstances, this can be regarded by some as the normal way of doing business. Assessors may experience this firsthand.

Ghost employees. This crime involves adding extra names to a company payroll and diverting the funds to a bank account specifically set up for this scam. Often, this is achieved by keeping an employee on the payroll after said employee has left the company.

Inflated invoices occur when a company inflates its bills without agreement from the bill payer, who may be a customer. Conversely, an employee may arrange to pay a vendor more than is due in return for an unauthorized payment or some other gain. Similarly, travel and entertainment (subsistence) claims occur when claims are falsified or inflated for personal gain, or there is basic abuse of the system for reimbursement claims. Similar are misappropriation schemes that are altering sales figures, writing off income that was actually received, obtaining blank purchase orders, amending documentation, diverting vendor discounts and writing off balances.

Money laundering is an important activity for most criminal activity. It is the securing of the proceeds of a criminal act. The proceeds must be integrated into the legal economy before the perpetrators can use it, so the purpose of laundering is to disguise the illegal origins of said proceeds. Money laundering takes place within all types of profit-motivated crimes, such as embezzlement, fraud, misappropriation, corruption, robbery, distribution of narcotics, and trafficking in human beings.

Income tax crime. The failure to comply with national income tax laws is one of the most prevalent financial crimes in many countries. The Internal Revenue Service in the United States estimates that the total individual tax gap in the nation is around $245 billion. Tax evasion can be divided into three main categories: undeclared work/business, unlawful planning and adjustment of taxes, and exploitation of ambiguities or alleged loopholes in the legislation so as to obtain improper tax advantages.

Corruption Crime

Corruption is defined as the giving, requesting, receiving, or accepting of an improper advantage related to a position, office, or assignment. The improper advantage does not have to be connected to a specific action or to not-performing this action. It is sufficient if the advantage can be linked to a person's position, office, or assignment. An individual or group is guilty of corruption if they accept payment in any form for doing something that they are obligated to do anyway or that they are prohibited from doing, or to exercise a legitimate action for improper reason. Corruption is also to destroy or pervert the integrity or fidelity of a person in his discharge of duty, to induce someone to act dishonestly or unfaithfully, to make venal, and to bribe.

Bribery is corruption conducted to achieve a favorable treatment. For example, the German bus manufacturer MAN suggested to Norwegian city officials that they specify a bus length of 18 meters and 75 centimeters in their next request for busses. City officials in Oslo did, and the only supplier who could deliver buses of that specific length was MAN. Volvo and other manufacturers could not. So MAN got the contract. In return, executives of public transportation firms in Oslo got money in cash handed over to them in German forests.

Kickbacks. An employee with influence over who gets a particular contract is able and willing to obtain something for assisting the prospective contractor. Likewise, bribes may be paid to inspectors to turn a blind eye to substandard goods coming into a loading dock. If bribes do not work, the dedicated fraudster may well turn to blackmail and pose threats.

Organizational corruption, the pursuit of interests by organizational actors through the intentional misdirection of organizational resources or perversion of organizational routines, might ultimately impede the organization's ability to accomplish its legitimate purpose and may threaten its very survival.

Public corruption is the abuse of entrusted power by political leaders for private gain. The corrosive effect of corruption undermines all efforts to improve governance and foster development. Corruption is just as much an economic problem as it is a political and social one, since it is a cancer that burdens the poor in developing countries.

Micro and Macro Views of Corruption

We are most accustomed to thinking about corrupt behavior in organizations primarily in micro level terms. Ashforth et al. (2008) argue that it is comforting to assume that one renegade faction within an organization is somewhat responsible for the corruption we too often observe. However, organizations are important to our understanding of corruption, because they influence the actions of their members. Therefore, both micro and macro views are important to understand corruption.

Pinto et al. (2008) applied both views in their study of corruption. They focused on two fundamental dimensions of corruption in organizations: (1) whether the individual or the organization is the beneficiary of the corrupt activity and (2) whether the corrupt behavior is undertaken by an individual actor or by two or more actors.

To enable a better understanding of the similarities, distinctions, frictions, and complementarities among corruption control types and to lay the groundwork for future study of their effectiveness in combination, Lange (2008) sets forth a theoretical basis for considering a corruption control type in the context of other corruption control types. Pfarrer et al. (2008) propose a four-stage model of the organizational actions that potentially increase the speed and likelihood that an organization will restore its legitimacy with stakeholders following a transgression. Misangyi et al. (2008) draw from theories of institutions and collective identities to present a threefold framework of institutional change involving institutional logic, resources, and social actors that furthers our understanding of the mitigation of corruption.

Corruption tends to have a deep impact on business corporations, business industries, and society as a whole. Corruption has an important economic as well as social impact. Dion (2010) describes corruption from three basic viewpoints: the structural perspective, the social-normative perspective, and the organizational-normative perspective. In the structural perspective, corruption is a local and domestic issue, so that the best way to get rid of it is to have stronger laws and regulations. In the social-normative perspective, corruption is common wherever most of the people have dishonest practices and customs. Corruption is not perceived as an immoral behavior, since it has been socially institutionalized and tolerated by political authorities. In the organizational-normative perspective, corruption is dependent on organizational norms of behavior and may take on three different forms, such as procedural corruption, schematic corruption, and categorical corruption.

Collins et al. (2009) studied why firms engage in corruption in India. Building on a survey of 341 executives in India, they found that if executives have social ties with government officials, their firms are more likely to engage in corruption. Also, these executives are likely to reason that engaging in corruption is a necessity for being competitive.

Auditing Role in Crime Detection

The role of auditing in the detection of white-collar crime is an interesting topic, as it is not obvious that auditors are able to detect crime. This might have to do with the responsibilities of auditing functions as well as procedures and practices followed by auditors in their work (Warhuus, 2011). For example, Beasley (2003) is concerned with the fact that auditors seem to struggle with reducing occurrences of material misstatements due to fraud, even in light of new standards for auditing. The focus of new standards remains on fraudulent activities that lead to intentional material misstatements due to fraud, and it expands the guidance and procedures to be performed in every audit. The expanded guidance might hopefully lead to improvements of auditor detection of material misstatements due to fraud by strengthening the auditor's responses to identified high fraud risks.

Samociuk and Iyer (2009) argue that fraud risks need recording, monitoring, and reporting. Recording includes the nature of each risk, likelihood and consequences, current and suggested controls, and the owner of the risk for follow-up action.

Moyes and Baker (2003) asked external, internal and governmental auditors to evaluate the effectiveness of various standard audit procedures in detecting fraud. Although external and internal auditors differed in the types of audit procedures they recommended, the authors concluded that "the audit procedures judged more effective in detecting fraud were those [that] provided evidence about the existence of internal controls and those [that] evaluated the strength of internal controls", and that "strategic use of standard audit procedures may help auditors fulfill their responsibilities under statement of auditing standards No. 99" (199). Further, "The results of this study indicate that fraud detection might be improved through the strategic use of standard audit procedures earlier in the audit examination. . . . If these audit procedures were applied during the preliminary stages of the audit, they would be more likely to indicate the potential existence of fraud, in which case the auditor would have more time to revise the audit plan and conduct other necessary investigations" (216).

Albrecht et al. (2001) "review the fraud detection aspects of current auditing standards and the empirical and other research that has been conducted on fraud detection." They conclude that "even though the red flag approach to detecting fraud has been endorsed by policy makers and written about widely by researchers, there is little empirical evidence that shows the red flag approach is an effective way to detect fraud, especially for fraud that has yet to be discovered" (4). Their research review on the subject reveals that one of the major conclusions drawn from previous studies include the fact that only 18 to 20 percent of fraud seems to be detected by internal and external auditors and further, that only about half of the perpetrators of fraud detected are prosecuted. The article also calls for further fraud detection research.

Low detection rates are loosely corroborated by Silverstone and Sheetz (2003), who estimate that approximately 12 percent of initial fraud detection is through external audit and approximately 19 percent is from internal audit. Both of these estimations apply to the American context.

An article by Farrell and Healy (2000) dealing with the responsibilities for prevention and detection of white-collar crime refers to a study undertaken to map how members of the accounting profession viewed the changing role of the external auditor following the introduction of statement of auditing standards No. 82. "Most of those answering the questionnaire disagreed that they should be responsible for searching for fraud. . . . Clearly, this notion concerning the auditor's responsibility is not widely held by the public at large. . . . The general public and Congress certainly sided against the CPAs [certified public accountants] and was the reason for this legislation." To the question of whether the CPAs should act as police or detectives when performing the audit, the response was a resounding no. "This may also indicate that changes brought about with the implementation of the SAS No. 82 requiring a *policing component* clearly require added responsibility and may necessitate additional training and changes to job description requirements. Again, although the general public may believe policing is within the auditors' duties, even SAS No. 82 does not require this" (25).

Similarly, an investigation by Johnson and Rudesill (2001) into fraud prevention and detection in the United States uncovered that the majority of CPAs who responded to the study "believe the external auditor's responsibility for fraud detection extends only to assessing the probability of fraud and planning the audit accordingly. They rank internal auditors the group most effective in detecting fraud, followed by fraud examiners and client management" (75).

M. Jones's 2009 article states:

> A persistent debate has dogged relationships between auditors and managers. This debate revolves around the precise roles and duties of each party in relation to fraud and corruption, and particularly who should take responsibility for investigation. Current legal and professional precedents leave little doubt that management bears the main responsibility for ensuring that reasonable measures are taken to prevent fraud and corruption. In any event it is common practice for managers to request assistance and advice from auditors upon suspicion or discovery of fraud. The final responsibility must lie with managers unless the auditor has given specific assurance regarding particular controls or the absence of error or fraud (12).

Within the extant accounting and auditing research, much attention is devoted to how the external auditor is a primary figure in detecting irregularities and corruption. Government and standard setters also stress the importance of the responsibilities of the auditing community in this respect. However, there seems to be limited faith and responsibility in the auditing function among some for this specific purpose: Only in very few cases does auditing in some form seem to be responsible for the detection, unraveling, and exposure of the offense. This opinion is backed by the work of Drage and Olstad (2008), who analyzed the role of the auditing function in relation to both preventing and detecting white-collar crime. Although their study included a look at the perceived preventative power of the auditing function as well as actual detection of criminal offenses, their findings were consistent with the previously mentioned hypothesis: Many of their interviewees were skeptical as to the auditing function having a central role in the detection of white-collar crime.

Olsen (2007) reminds us that the auditing standards with which the external auditors must comply also require them to uncover irregularities should they be present. However, the primary concern of the external auditor is to reduce the auditing risk (i.e., the risk that the financial statements may still contain material misstatements even after the auditor has given a positive auditor report), not the risk of irregularities. In spite of external auditors rarely being credited for the detection of financial crime, Olsen (2007) still believes that the auditing function contributes significantly to the prevention of such crime by reducing temptations and opportunities, thus corroborating the findings of Drage and Olstad (2008) on prevention.

Rendal and Westerby (2010) examined Norwegian auditors' expectations toward their own abilities in detecting and preventing irregularities and compared these with the expectations other users of financial information have toward this same issue. Their findings indicate certain gaps in how the auditor is expected to perform. Auditors themselves admit that they sometimes do not act in accordance with laws and regulations, and both auditors and users of financial information feel that the auditing function should include more than what is required today through standards and regulations. They also uncover unrealistic expectations regarding the extent to which the auditing function is capable of uncovering irregularities. They conclude that auditors, to a certain extent, are too reserved and aloof when it comes to their responsibilities in the prevention and detection of irregularities, and call for improvements.

The Case of Hermansen at Spitsbergen

Robert Hermansen, age 74, the former Norwegian chairman and chief executive officer of the world's northernmost mining company, Store Norske Spitsbergen Kullkompani, was sentenced in 2011 to two years in prison for his role in a bribery scandal at the Svalbard firm. He also faces huge debt after being ordered to repay nearly NOK (Norwegian kroner) 4 million (USD 700,000) in what the court in Nord-Troms viewed as bribes from the Bergen-based shipping company Kristian Jebsens Rederi. Jebsens enjoyed expensive long-term contracts to ship ore from the mines that were tied to payments to Hermansen.

Hermansen, who had enjoyed a long career as a businessman before the bribery charges were filed, confessed to receiving the money from Jebsens but told newspaper *Dagens Næringsliv (The Norwegian Business Daily)* that he thought his sentence was much too strict. He was considering an appeal but said he didn't fear going to jail.

"I've never been in prison before, it will be a new experience," he told DN. "Most experiences are worth something."

Hermansen was once one of Svalbard's greatest modern-day heroes. He turned the coal company from being a heavily subsidized state company into a profitable venture. There is even a bust of him in the city of Longyearbyen on Norway's Arctic archipelago of Svalbard. But he admitted to accepting a total of NOK 4 million from the shipping company that transported Store Norske's coal from Svalbard, Kristian Jebsens Rederi, in return for dropping any bidding for the job. Jebsens secured what a consulting company hired in by Store Norske after Hermansen retired in 2008 called "remarkably long-term and expensive" contracts.

An investigation was launched in 2010 into Hermansen's dealings with Jebsens, resulting in bribery charges and his confession and conviction in 2011. "This is a relief, really, for Hermansen and for many others," his lawyer Frode Sulland told news bureau NTB. "He's humble and willing to take the punishment the court will hand out."

Hermansen had a long and distinguished career before heading for Svalbard 20 years ago. He is the brother of Tormod Hermansen, the former chief executive of telecoms giant Telenor (Østerbø, K., 2013).

The Case of Røkke at Aker

Kjell Inge Røkke, one of Norway's most successful businessmen and industrialists, was spending his days in jail in Vestfold, south of Oslo, in 2007. Røkke, convicted of bribery in bypassing standard procedure to obtain a boating license, was sentenced in 2005 to 120 days in prison. He appealed but dropped it when an appeals court agreed to hear parts of his case that related to the length of his sentence. Røkke, 48 at the time, only spent about 30 days in actual custody, however, since 90 days of his jail term were suspended. Røkke's attorney Ellen Holager Andenæs told the newspaper *Aftenposten* that her client thus did not see any point in moving forward with the appeal, and would accept his sentence even though he maintained his innocence (Hanssen, 2007).

Røkke, who built his fortune fishing off the coast of Alaska, needed the license to operate a large pleasure craft he was acquiring. *Dagens Næringsliv*, however, published a series of articles suggesting that Røkke obtained the license via unconventional means. The articles led to an investigation, and Røkke and his butler were ultimately convicted of fraud and delivering false testimony. In addition, a Swedish maritime inspector was convicted of receiving bribes along with a Norwegian yacht broker.

White-Collar Crime Cases

Every year, an average of 100 white-collar criminals are sentenced to prison in Norway. Based on newspaper reports and court documents, a database of more than 300 convicted criminals is applied in this research to answer the following research question: What predicts the prison sentence in terms of years in jail for main criminals in white-collar crime cases? The sampling procedure for the research database is presented in chapter 8, where an empirical study of white-collar lawyers is presented.

Two significant predictors were identified for prison sentence in terms of years in jail for the main criminal. First, the amount of money involved in the crime has a significant impact on court sentence. Second, the number of people involved in the crime has a significant impact on court sentence for the primary criminal. This research is important, as it presents statistical evidence for white-collar crime research, while most other studies only present anecdotal evidence from well-known single white-collar crime cases. Two other potential determinants of jail sentence were identified, as illustrated in Figure 1.2: size of organization and age of criminal.

White-collar crime is concerned with financial crime, where an illegal profit is achieved by gaining access to values that belonged to someone else. In tax fraud, the money stolen belongs to society; in bank fraud, the money belongs to the bank. With insider trading, the money belongs to other shareholders. If the amount of money is large, then a more severe jail sentence may be expected in court.

Hypothesis 1: A greater amount of money involved in financial crime will lead to a longer jail sentence for the main criminal.

Some financial crime cases involve only one person, who is typically labeled a rotten apple. Most cases, however, involve more

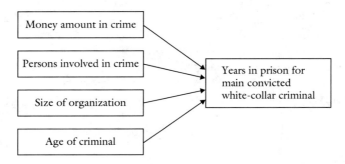

Figure 1.2 Potential predictors of jail sentence in white-collar crime cases

individuals, where typically one of the individuals takes on a leadership role. It is expected that the leader as the main criminal will receive a more severe jail sentence if several persons are participating as followers in the crime.

Hypothesis 2: A larger number of persons involved in financial crime will lead to a longer jail sentence for the main criminal.

In larger organizations, it can be easier to cover up unethical and illegal activities. If an organizational member is prosecuted for financial crime, it can be expected that the white-collar criminal is blaming culture, systems, and procedures for his wrongdoing. Therefore, individuals in larger organizations can expect shorter jail sentences when compared to individuals in smaller organizations.

Hypothesis 3: Financial crime committed in a larger organization will lead to a shorter jail sentence for the main criminal.

In white-collar crime, the offender is typically older than an average street criminal. Age can be a factor that influences court decisions, because older, well-established individuals will have an even less plausible or acceptable motive for financial crime. If an older white-collar offender is prosecuted in court, the jail sentence will be longer than when a younger white-collar offender is prosecuted in court.

Hypothesis 4: An older main criminal will receive a longer jail sentence.

Based on newspaper reports, a total of 342 white-collar criminals were convicted for white-collar crime from 2009 to 2012 in 163 criminal court cases with an average of 2.1 persons involved in each case. Prison sentenced reached from a minimum of a few weeks to a maximum of 9 years. The amount of money in terms of Norwegian kroner ranged from less than 1 million to a maximum of NOK 1.2 billion, where six Norwegian kroner is equal to one US dollar. The number of involved persons ranged from 1 to a maximum of 16 criminals in a case. Organizational size where the criminal(s) performed their professional activities ranged from 1 employee to 2000 employees. Criminal age ranged from 17 years to a maximum of 75 years in the database at the time of conviction in court.

As listed in Table 1.1, the average sentence was 2.7 years in jail, 41 million Norwegian kroner involved in the crime, 2.1 persons on average involved in the criminal activity, the business organization where the criminal(s) belonged had 112 employees, and the average age of the main criminal was 48 years.

Correlation analysis in the table indicates strong covariations between years in prison and amount of money involved, prison sentence and number of persons involved, and organization size and age of perpetrator. A larger money amount involved in the crime is associated with a longer jail sentence. A larger number of persons involved in the crime are associated with a longer jail sentence. An older criminal is associated with a larger organization in terms of people employed.

To test our four research hypotheses, regression analysis is needed, where four independent variables are potential predictors of one dependent variable. The dependent variable is prison sentence, while four independent variables are money, persons, organization, and age. Results for the total regression equation are listed in Table 1.2. R^2 represents the extent to which our four independent variables are able to explain variation in the dependent variable. With an adjusted R^2 of .404, our four independent variables are able to explain 40 percent of the variation in prison sentence.

Table 1.1 Correlation coefficients for crime variables (statistical significance is measured in terms of probability of possible mistake, where mistake is .05 at * and .01 at **)

	Average	Deviation	Prison	Money	Persons	Size	Age
Years in prison	2.7	2.1	1	.463**	.506**	.047	.090
Money in millions	41	231		1	.146	.005	.152
Persons involved	2.1	2.1			1	.066	−.130
Size organization	112	266				1	.220**
Age main criminal	48	12					1

Table 1.2 Regression analysis for research model

Model Summary				
Model	R	R^2	Adjusted R^2	Std. Error of the Estimate
1	.647[a]	.419	.404	1.61685

a. Predictors: (Constant), Age, Persons Involved, Money, Size

Table 1.3 Significance of regression equation

		ANOVA[a]				
	Model	Sum of Squares	df	Mean Square	F	Sig.
1	Regression	298.106	4	74.526	28.508	.000[b]
	Residual	413.043	158	2.614		
	Total	711.149	162			

a. Dependent Variable: Prison
b. Predictors: (Constant), Age, Persons Involved, Money, Size

Table 1.4 Significance of each predictor variable in regression analysis (Constant means starting point of a line for regression equation)

		Coefficients[a]				
		Unstandardized Coefficients		Standardized Coefficients	t	Sig.
Model		B	Std. Error	Beta		
1	(Constant)	.676	.584		1.157	.249
	Money	.006	.001	.381	6.117	.000
	Involved	.452	.061	.463	7.424	.000
	Size	-4.669E-.005	.000	-.006	-.095	.925
	Age	.017	.011	.094	1.468	.144

a. Dependent Variable: Prison

As indicated in Table 1.3, our regression equation with four predictor variables is significant at the level of .000.

As indicated in Table 1.4, not all four predictor variables are significant in the regression equation. Only money amount and involved persons are significant predictors, while size and age are not.

In terms of hypotheses testing, Hypothesis 1 and Hypotheses 2 were confirmed, while Hypothesis 3 and Hypothesis 4 were not validated.

2
White-Collar Crime Defense Lawyers

Lawyers are skilled in knowing general legal principles, procedures, and substantive aspects of the law; thus they have the ability to analyze and provide solutions to legal problems (Dibbern et al., 2008). Lawyers, as knowledge workers, apply a variety of knowledge categories, such as declarative and procedural knowledge. Most lawyers spend several hours a day answering the types of queries that cannot be captured or researched in a general knowledge base. As part of the execution of knowledge processes, lawyers can decide for themselves what knowledge they want to evaluate, develop, implement, and communicate in relation to their cases. When several lawyers work on the same case, there is often an independence of professionals working together, which might be characterized as collective individualism or individualistic collectivism that makes the sharing of knowledge both dynamic and random. Autonomy of performance is an important structural feature that can promote knowledge processes, since such autonomy encourages individuals to develop new knowledge. At the same time, several people looking at the same problem can come up with different, novel approaches to solving the problem. Lawyers, as knowledge professionals with a great deal of autonomy, are free to choose an individual approach to knowledge processes, including the need for, storage of, access to, sharing of, application of, creation of, and evaluation of knowledge as they relate to their cases.

Characteristics of White-Collar Lawyers

A white-collar crime lawyer (WCC lawyer) is a defense attorney in criminal court cases that are concerned with financial crime. Both knowledge and behavior of WCC lawyers distinguish them for other defense roles. A WCC lawyer's knowledge is about business insights, understanding of economics, experience in reading accounting statements, and knowledge of tax regulations and other laws and regulations related to financial crime.

Lawyer behavior in WCC cases is different from other cases, for example, in terms of resources and in terms of ambiguity regarding whether the action in question was not just unethical, but also illegal. Breaking rules is different from violating laws, and there is often significant uncertainty whether a white-collar suspect has done something that may lead the person to imprisonment. Furthermore, there are challenging tasks related to facts. In a murder case, the facts are usually quite clear: A person is killed and found dead. In a financial crime case, the facts are not that obvious, as financial transactions can have different purposes and justifications.

While the judge in these cases is typically a generalist, the lawyer is a specialist. Simply stated, a generalist is a person who knows little about a lot, while a specialist is a person who knows a lot about a little. When the WCC lawyer defends an executive or shareholder in court, the lawyer is on his home field, while the judge is often unfamiliar with factual as well as legal issues in the case. On the day before, the judge may have passed a verdict in a child abuse case, a murder case, or a traffic violation case. The lawyer, however, may have helped another WCC client in a similar financial case the day before.

Gillers (2012) argues that specialization in legal fields is a complement to the movement toward conformity of law. Specialization will make each lawyer better able to gain competency with the law in the area of specialization. Specialists know what variations to look for. Specialization is increasingly defined by expertise in areas of law. Specialized knowledge will often define the borders of a lawyer's competence with greater assurance than will geographical borders of the clients.

A concept might be defined in its own right or in terms of difference from other concepts. For example, a man could be defined as such, or as different from a woman. In themselves, white-collar lawyers are characterized by their clients, who are white-collar criminals. Similar terminology is used for celebrity lawyers and divorce lawyers, who have clients of fame and clients of marriage breakdown, respectively. In this case, it is the client who defines the lawyer.

Lawyers are often defined in terms of their area of expertise. Some are tax lawyers, while others are merger-and-acquisition lawyers or maritime lawyers. A white-collar crime lawyer can work in several legal areas, as long as the client is a white-collar suspect. For example, white-collar crime cases may range from tax fraud via accounting fraud to corruption.

Attanasio (2008) argues that there are a number of issues where a knowledgeable defense lawyer can help the WCC client early on in the process:

> One of the most pressing challenges facing white-collar crime defense counsel early in an investigation is to persuade an intelligent, successful, and proactive client to engage in what he or she will likely think is counterintuitive behavior. Many executives, however, wind up in federal prisons not because of the conduct that was initially being investigated—but because of statements they made afterwards to government agents or even to co-workers and friends (all of whom are potential witnesses once an investigation is underway). One of the most common mistakes that a white-collar target can make is to think that "all of this will end if I can just tell everybody what really happened" (58).

Similarly, there are a number of issues where the knowledgeable defense lawyer can help the white-collar crime client late in the process. If the client is convicted and given a prison sentence, then the lawyer may help ease conditions during imprisonment. The lawyer may argue by the special sensitivity hypothesis, which claims that white-collar offenders are ill-equipped to adjust to the rigors of prison life (Stadler et al., 2013):

> Termed the "special sensitivity hypothesis," the claim is made that white-collar offenders experience the pains of imprisonment to a greater degree than traditional street offenders. Upon incarceration, they enter a world that is foreign to them. In the society of captives, status hierarchies found in the larger community are upended, as those with more physical prowess and criminal connections "rule the joint". White-collar offenders discover that they are no longer in the majority in a domain populated largely by poor and minority group members—in fact, prison is a place that a researcher suggests is the functional equivalent of an urban ghetto (2).

Furthermore, Stadler et al. found that research investigating the sentencing of white-collar offenders has revealed that federal judges often base their decisions not to impose a prison sentence for white-collar offenses on the belief that prison is both unnecessary for and unduly harsh on white-collar offenders.

Even when white-collar crime lawyers argue the case of special sensitivity for their clients, Stadler et al. found that the historical pattern of lenient treatment of white-collar offenders appears to be waning. Following widespread public outrage and condemnation of white-collar criminals in regions such as Northern Europe and North America for the lavish lifestyles, unscrupulous deeds, and fraudulent actions of corporate executives and stock market acrobats, the prosecution and imprisonment of white-collar criminals has become increasingly common.

Furthermore, the special sensitivity hypothesis for white-collar criminals sometimes argued by their personal lawyers is not necessarily true. In research conducted by Stadler et al., they found that white-collar inmates were in fact better at prison adjustment, experienced fewer difficulties in prison, had less trouble sleeping, had less need of safety in prison, experienced fewer problems with current and former cellmates, and made easier friends in prison than other inmates in the prison.

A challenge for white-collar crime lawyers is sometimes the lack of guilt perceived by their clients (Stadler and Benson, 2012):

> Indeed, a distinguishing feature of the psychological makeup of white-collar offenders is thought to be their ability to neutralize the moral bind of the law and rationalize their criminal behavior (494).

In the United States, it is argued that white-collar sentencing has been strengthened after the devastating collapse of Enron and other major American corporations such as WorldCom, Tyco, and Xerox. Congress enacted the Sarbanes-Oxley Act, which was passed hastily by a seemingly shaken legislature. The Act included a multitude of reforms aimed at preventing another meltdown (Harvard Law Review, 2009):

> One particular area of reform was white collar criminal sentencing: included in the Act was the White-Collar Crime Penalty Enhancement Act of 2002 (WCCPA), which sharply increased penalties for various forms of fraud (1728).

Lawyers as Knowledge Workers

Basic knowledge is required for a lawyer as a professional to understand and interpret information, and basic knowledge is required for a law firm as a knowledge organization to receive inputs and produce outputs (Galanter and Palay, 1991). Advanced knowledge is knowledge necessary to get acceptable work done (Zack, 1999). Advanced knowledge is required for a lawyer as a knowledge worker to achieve satisfactory work performance, and advanced knowledge is required for a law firm as a knowledge organization to produce legal advice and legal documents that are acceptable to clients. When advanced knowledge is combined with basic knowledge, then we find professional knowledge workers and professional knowledge organizations in the legal industry (Mountain, 2001; Nottage, 1998; Phillips, 2005). Innovative knowledge is knowledge that makes a real difference. When lawyers apply innovative knowledge in analysis and reasoning based on incoming and available information, then new insights and possible novel solutions are generated in terms of situation patterns, actor profiles, and client strategies. Knowledge levels here were defined based on Parsons 2004 work.

An alternative approach is to define knowledge levels in terms of knowledge depth: know-what, know-how, and know-why, respectively. These knowledge depth levels represent the extent of insight and understanding about a phenomenon.

Know-what is knowledge about what is happening and what is going on. A lawyer perceives that something is going on that might need attention. The lawyer's insight is limited to the perception of something happening. The lawyer understands neither how it is happening nor why it is happening.

Know-how is a lawyer's knowledge about how a legal case develops, how a criminal behaves, how investigations can be carried out, or how a criminal business enterprise is organized. The lawyer's insight is not limited to the perception that something is happening; she also understands how it is happening or how "it is." Similarly, know-how is present when the lawyer understands how legal work is to be carried out and how the client will react to advice put forward in the process.

Know-why is the knowledge representing the deepest form of understanding and insights into a phenomenon. The lawyer does not only know that it has occurred and how it has occurred, but she also has developed an understanding of why it has occurred or why it is like this. It is a matter of causal understanding where cause-and-effect relationships are understood.

A law firm is a business entity formed by one or more lawyers to engage in the practice of law. Most law firms use a partnership form of organization. In such a framework, lawyers who are highly effective in using and applying knowledge for fee earnings are eventually rewarded with partner status and thus own a stake in the firm, resulting in an income often ten times as much as their starting salaries. While a newly hired law graduate might make 100,000 USD, a partner might make 1,000,000 USD.

In many countries, lawyers and law firms enjoy privileges that make them attractive to white-collar criminals and crime. For example, money placed in a client account at a Norwegian law firm is strictly confidential. The law firm does not have to tell tax or other authorities about names or amounts. Knowing that some of this money flows freely to and from tax havens like the Cayman Islands and knowing that some of the money originates from white-collar crime makes the job of the prosecution extremely difficult (Vanvik, 2011).

Another example is Danish law firms where there is an "in kassu" system. Many in kassus are run by law firms, and they buy debts and chase debtors for many companies in Denmark. The reason is that unlike non-law firms, they are authorized and not subject to regulation. The only way a complaint can be filed is through the lawyers' association, where a board of lawyers provides self-regulation on behalf of all lawyers (Trustpilot, 2013).

Iossa and Jullien (2012) distinguish between higher-quality and lower-quality lawyers. The first category comprises lawyers who graduated from elite institutions, serve business clients, and charge high fees. Here we typically find knowledgeable white-collar crime lawyers. The second category serves more individual clients and comprises lawyers who graduated from lower-tier schools, charge lower fees, and provide largely routine, noncontested legal services. Depending on their category, lawyers are then employed in different law firms, with the most reputable firms employing the most talented and well-trained lawyers.

Knowledge Competition in Court

From a legal perspective, a court situation is characterized by efforts to conclude whether the charged persons and/or company are guilty or not guilty. From a knowledge perspective, this situation is characterized by a competition as illustrated in Figure 2.1.

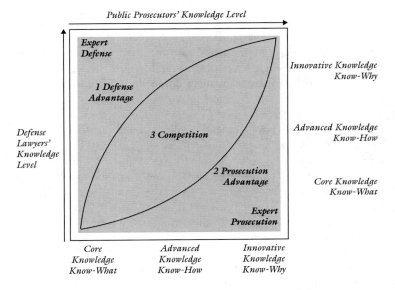

Figure 2.1 Knowledge rivalry between prosecution and defense in court

Depending on the relative knowledge levels of prosecution and defense, a knowledge rivalry with three alternative situations might exist as illustrated in Figure 2.1:

1. Defense lawyers are experts, while prosecutors are not experts in areas such as international tax regulations, tax havens, global company operations, and management of international operations. Defense lawyers have innovative knowledge (know-why), while prosecutors have core knowledge (know-what).
2. Prosecutors are experts, while defense lawyers are not experts in Norwegian laws and regulations. Defense lawyers have core knowledge (know-what), while prosecutors have innovative knowledge (know-why).
3. Both parties are at about the same knowledge level, leading to a real knowledge competition in court between the defense lawyers and prosecutors.

In Norway, street criminals such as burglars and rapists seldom can afford several top defense lawyers for weeks and months in court, but white-collar criminals often can. This discrepancy emphasizes the importance of Sutherland's (1949) seminal work on white-collar crime. The most economically disadvantaged members of society are not the only ones committing crime. Members of the privileged socioeconomic class are also engaged in criminal behavior (Brightman, 2009; Croall, 2007), and the types of crime may differ from those of the lower classes. Some examples of the former are business executives bribing public officials to obtain contracts, chief accountants manipulating balance sheets to avoid taxes, and procurement managers approving fake invoices for personal gain (Simpson and Weisburd, 2009). The elements of competition and rivalry make practicing law an entrepreneurial endeavor, but ultimately defense lawyers have an advantage in that they know the full extent of their clients' guilt. The lawyer has insider knowledge.

Criminal behavior by members of the privileged socioeconomic class is routinely labeled white-collar crime when financial crime occurs (Benson and Simpson, 2009; Simpson, 2011). As mentioned earlier, Sutherland (1949), in his seminal work, defined white-collar crime as crime committed by a person of respectability and high social status in the course of his occupation. According to Brightman (2009), Sutherland's theory of white-collar crime from 1939 was controversial, particularly since many of the academics in the audience perceived themselves to be members of the upper echelon of American society, where white-collar criminals can be found. Despite his critics, Sutherland's theory of white-collar criminality served as the catalyst for an area of research that continues today. In particular, differential association theory proposes that a person associating with individuals who have deviant or unlawful mores, values, and norms learns criminal behavior. Certain characteristics play a key role in placing individuals in a position to act illegally. These include the proposition that criminal behavior is learned through interaction with other criminal persons in the upper echelon and the interaction that occurs in small intimate groups who might be involved in corruption, money laundering, or embezzlement (Hansen, 2009).

Sutherland argued that white-collar criminal acts are illegalities that are contingently differentiated from other illegalities by virtue of the specific administrative procedures to which they are subject. Some individual white-collar offenders avoid criminal prosecution because of the class bias of the courts (Tombs and Whyte, 2007). As a consequence, white-collar crime is sometimes considered creative crime (Brisman, 2010) and something to be grudgingly admired.

As part of the white-collar criminal definition, the role of class has been highly contested because the status of an offender may matter less than the harm done by someone in a trusted occupational position. Croall (2007) argues that the term "crime" is also contentious, since many of the harmful activities of businesses or occupational groups are not subject to criminal law and punishment but to administrative or regulatory law and penalties and sanctions. Therefore, some have suggested a definition of white-collar crime as an abuse of a legitimate occupational role that is regulated by law, typically representing a violation of trust. It is also apparent that white-collar defense lawyers are predominantly drawn from the elite too. Indeed, Osiel (1990) referred to a class of lawyers as being monopolists, aristocrats, and entrepreneurs.

White-Collar Crime Law Firms

Attorneys who defend white-collar criminals are sometimes labeled "white-collar crime lawyers," "white-collar defense attorneys," or simply "white-collar lawyers." Some entire law firms have specialized in white-collar crime cases. Here is how a firm named White & Case presents itself on the Internet (http://www.whitecase.com/whitecollar/):

> The White Collar Practice offers clients around the world first-rate skills in dealing with government investigations and enforcement matters. Our lawyers have substantial experience defending clients through all phases of investigations as well as criminal and civil enforcement proceedings. These capabilities are enhanced by the resources of a preeminent international law firm, including local law proficiency and familiarity with local enforcement authorities in major business centers around the world. Clients include large corporations, banks, and other institutions, as well as individuals prominent in business and political affairs.
>
> The White Collar group serves clients around the world in civil and criminal matters. The common element is the involvement of a government agency engaged in fact-gathering or enforcement proceedings. The group is prepared to defend the interests of domestic and international clients, offering them immediate access to high-caliber legal counsel with substantial experience in complex as well as controversial matters. These include financial fraud, public and private corruption, money-laundering, securities fraud, environmental, tax, and antitrust cases.

One of the white-collar cases handled by White & Case LLP was referenced in the *Harvard Law Review*, volume 124, in 2011. The case was concerned with courts authorized to issue protective orders limiting disclosure of evidence produced in civil discovery.

Another example of a white-collar law firm is Covington & Burling, who apply the term "white collar lawyers" to themselves and who present their defense competence in white-collar crime cases on the Internet (http://www.cov.com/practice/white_collar_and_investigations/):

> Our white collar lawyers successfully represent both corporations and individuals in criminal and regulatory investigations by the U.S. Department of Justice, federal regulatory agencies, and state and local prosecutors and regulators throughout the nation. Covington's White Collar Defense & Investigations Practice is widely recognized not only for litigating and winning high-profile criminal cases, but also for devising creative legal strategies to resolve cases long before they draw public scrutiny. Covington's long-standing record of excellence in defending clients in complex criminal and regulatory enforcement cases has earned the firm a deep and invaluable reservoir of credibility with courts, prosecutors and regulatory agencies nationwide.
>
> Our white collar practice includes 30 partners, most of whom are former prosecutors and SEC enforcement attorneys who have held senior positions in United States Attorney's Offices, the U.S. Department of Justice, the White House, the Securities and Exchange Commission, and other government agencies involved in white collar criminal and regulatory enforcement.

The Transocean Court Case

Transocean, one of the world's largest offshore contractors of drilling rigs, is accused of having underpaid taxes by up to 10 billion Norwegian kroner (USD 1.8 billion) from 2000 to 2002 according to Økokrim, the police unit that investigates economic crime in Norway. Also known as the Norwegian National Authority for Investigation and Prosecution of Economic and Environmental Crime, Økokrim is similar to the Serious Fraud Office in the UK or the FBI in the United States.

Police say the alleged underpayments stem from several transactions in connection with the sale of 12 oil rigs from Transocean's Norwegian subsidiary to other company units in the Cayman Islands. Managing and manipulating assets in order to pay the lowest amount of taxes is a key part of Transocean's strategy, since its rigs move between jurisdictions; "It is common in the oil rig business," says Stephen L. Hayes, executive vice president of tax matters at Transocean. After growing to become the world's largest drilling contractor via three acquisitions of rivals worth $27 billion in the decade to 2009, the company moved its base to Switzerland from the Caymans for tax reasons. The company, which had operational headquarters in Houston before the Swiss move, has also shifted assets between subsidiaries over the years, which is at the heart of the Norwegian case (Klesty and Reddall, 2011).

Norwegian authorities indicted two companies owned by Transocean Ltd. and three tax advisers hired by Transocean over suspicions of tax fraud.

> "From 1996/97, the Transocean Group's master plan was to concentrate the ownership of the Group's Norwegian rigs in companies registered in the Cayman Islands," Økokrim said in the 24-page indictment. "The final decision in the Norway tax case was to be made by a Norwegian court," said Morten Eriksen, a lawyer for Økokrim. Transocean denied the allegations and said it intended to clear its name in court. "The indictment is based on an inadequate comprehension of the facts," defense counsel Erling O. Lyngtveit said in the statement. "Moreover in our opinion Økokrim base their conclusions on peculiar and original interpretation of Norwegian and international tax legislation." (Klesty and Reddall, 2011)

By December 5, 2012, when the case was brought against Transocean in Oslo District Court, it was the largest tax evasion case in Norwegian history. Prosecutors claimed that tax advisors for Transocean must have known they were misleading tax authorities. Raids on Transocean's offices in Stavanger, Norway, and years of investigation by Økokrim led to the firm, its advisers, and its affiliates being charged with evading taxes. Prosecutors claimed that Transocean's tax planning was managed in detail from its Houston headquarters, with Norwegian tax advisers at Ernst & Young as central players. A tax attorney at Oslo law firm Thommessen was also involved in the case, but local Transocean management in Norway was not believed to have been involved. Prosecutors claimed the alleged tax evasion was conducted from Houston headquarters (News from Norway, 2012).

The case was scheduled to last for 8 months.

A total of 29 persons were presented in court:

- public prosecutor Morten Eriksen with four associates (5 persons)
- the six Transocean executives from the USA accused of tax fraud, with six defense lawyers (12 persons)
- accused lawyer Sverre E. Koch, prosecuted for tax fraud advice, with three defense lawyers (4 persons)
- accused lawyer Klaus Klausen, prosecuted for tax fraud advice, with three defense lawyers (4 persons)
- accused lawyer Einar Brask, prosecuted for tax fraud advice, with three defense lawyers (4 persons).

It was estimated that the accused persons and Transocean itself would pay about $10 million for their defense lawyers, even though defense can be obtained for free in Norwegian courts. It is interesting to note that the prosecution had only 17 percent of the engaged personnel in the court room. In addition to the prosecution and defense, there were 3 judges in the district court on this case, making a total of 32 persons in court for 8 months.

While street criminals such as burglars and rapists seldom can afford several top defense lawyers for weeks and months in court, white-collar criminals often can. This discrepancy emphasizes the importance of seminal 1949 work on white-collar crime. The most economically disadvantaged members of society are not the only ones committing crime. Members of the privileged socioeconomic class are also engaged in criminal behavior (Brightman, 2009), and the types of crime they commit may differ from those of the lower classes. Tax evasion, as in the Transocean case, is an example of that type of crime and the class of criminal who can afford top-dollar defense.

The district court ruling in the Transocean case is expected in 2014. But it is also expected that the case will move on into a court of appeals. It is possible the Norwegian Supreme Court may consider a final judgment in the Transocean case in 2016 or 2017. This research is not concerned with whether or not the persons and the company are guilty as charged. Rather, this paper has presented the knowledge management view on white-collar crime cases, where white-collar criminals can afford a much better defense than street-level criminals. This discrepancy emphasizes the importance of the white-collar crime concept as defined by Sutherland (1940, 1949, 1983). The agency theory further emphasizes the role importance of principal (criminal) and agent (lawyer) for privileged white-collar criminals.

The Attorney-Client Privilege

The attorney-client privilege is one of the oldest privileges known to the common law in the United States. The privilege ensures that a client may provide information to his or her attorney, in confidence, with the knowledge that such information is protected, and neither the client nor the attorney may be forced to disclose the information that has been shared to their judicial adversaries (Kopon and Sungaila, 2012). Similar privilege exists between clients and attorneys in most other democratic societies. The privilege may extend to information concerning money, when a client has placed an amount in a law firm account. If the police suspect the money has originated from criminal activity or it is suspected that the money has been moved illegally to tax havens, the attorney-client privilege allows the attorney to deny the police access to accounts or information about the accounts. The attorney-client privilege shields from discovery any information communicated to an attorney to enable the attorney to render legal advice (Oh, 2004).

An attorney's ability to advise a client is directly dependent upon that client's willingness to engage in such full and truth-oriented communication. According to Kopon and Sungaila (2012), the privilege serves both the immediate needs of the individual client and public ends by ensuring sound and fully-informed legal advice and advocacy.

An attorney has both the ethical duty of confidentiality as well as the attorney-client privilege. The former is a rule of professional responsibility. The latter is an evidentiary privilege. Both principles seek to permit clients to control confidences shared their lawyers. Professional responsibility generally prohibits a lawyer from knowingly revealing a confidence or secret to the client's disadvantage without that client's consent (Bryans, 2009).

The Attorney-Client Asymmetry

There is an asymmetry in knowledge between the lawyer and the client. The lawyer is an expert on laws, verdicts, and legal procedures. The client is an expert on business transactions, management, and leadership. Knowledge asymmetry can benefit and hinder defense work. It can benefit defense work by combining knowledge and creating knowledge synergies. It can hinder defense work because of misunderstandings when there is a lack of minimum knowledge overlap between attorney and client.

Susskind (2010) emphasizes another kind of asymmetry between the commercial interest of law firms and those of their clients. In the ordinary course of events, when a client needs help from a lawyer, the client generally hopes that the involvement of the lawyer and the resultant fee can be kept to a bare minimum. Most clients would prefer to minimize legal expenses.

3

White-Collar Crime Defense Strategies

Three themes are particularly noteworthy when distinguishing white-collar crime defense strategies from other defense strategies for lawyers. First, the role of white-collar criminal lawyers is radically different from the typical criminal lawyer who defends persons charged with street crime. For instance, the former spend far more time on each case, both in terms of workload and in terms of calendar time. This implies that a white-collar crime lawyer works on fewer cases in parallel. The white-collar lawyer gets a case much earlier and is far more likely to keep charges from being filed. Second, information control is at the center of the white-collar crime attorney's work. The lawyer is concerned with acquisition of crucial information and keeps damaging information out of the hands of police investigators and public prosecutors. A third theme centers on a major dilemma of these lawyers: how to vigorously defend the client without thereby becoming a party to the criminal act (Kiser, 1986).

In line with these themes, three specific strategies applied by white-collar crime attorneys can be identified. First, a substance defense strategy is concerned with when and how an attorney decides to defend the client in a substantive way. Often, the substantive defense starts at a much earlier stage than in a street-crime case. Second, information control strategy is concerned with what and how crucial information is controlled to make it difficult, and sometimes impossible, for the police and prosecution to get the complete picture. Often, information control defense is able to keep secrets and to claim that pieces of information are irrelevant. In police investigations, there are normally a number of information sources, often more than a dozen, as we shall see in this chapter. Controlling and limiting some sources can ensure the crime puzzle is never solved in police investigations. Third, the symbolic defense strategy addresses all other means that the attorney can apply to divert attention away from legal issues. An example is to use the press or other media to portray the offender as a victim.

This chapter is mainly based on research at Yale University documented in the Yale Studies on White-Collar Crime series. One book is about white-collar crime lawyers. The book, *Defending White-Collar Crime: A Portrait of Attorneys at Work* written by Kenneth Mann and published by Yale University Press in 1985, is a true classic in white-collar crime research. As a classic research book, it is still relevant in its analysis of lawyers. Kenneth Mann's book is based on interviews with a number of white-collar crime attorneys, while this book is based on a statistical sample of more than three hundred white-collar criminals' attorneys.

As is the case in this chapter, the starting point for Mann is that white-collar crime defense is significantly different from other kinds of crime defense. A defense lawyer in a white-collar case spends much more time on the case itself and on each single case, both in terms of total workload and in terms of total calendar time. Therefore, a white-collar lawyer will work on far fewer cases in parallel as compared to a street-crime lawyer. The white-collar lawyer spends much more energy on information control to prevent authorities from obtaining crucial information that can harm the client. In addition, there is a dilemma for the lawyer when working with a client coming from the same middle class or upper class in society, with those types of clients being traditionally more resourceful than the attorney.

Substance Defense Strategy

The counterpart for an attorney in crime cases are the authorities, who decide whether a suspect shall be prosecuted or not. To prevent a prosecution decision, the defense lawyer will try to convince the police and prosecuting attorneys that the client has done nothing that justifies court proceedings. The strategic issue for the attorney is how to succeed in stopping the prosecutor from advancing the investigation from suspicion to prosecution in court. While very different from other crime cases, an attorney's active defense work often starts in the initial phases of a police investigation, when there are only rumors of wrongdoing that may or may not be relevant for criminal law. Initially it does not matter for the attorney whether the client has actually committed a crime, because rumors so often develop into accusations from colleagues, subordinates, management, customers, suppliers, journalists, or authorities. For example, a whistle-blower may continue to feed auditors and the police as well as the media with information about the suspect. Some of the information might be true, while other information might be false. Therefore, the attorney must initially try to sort all this information into a picture of threats for the client and the future defense work.

If a white-collar attorney were to behave in white-collar cases as attorneys in street-crime cases, then the attorney would wait for evidence to be presented against the client. Then the attorney would react to the evidence. A street-crime lawyer is mainly reactive, while a white-collar lawyer is proactive. A street-crime lawyer waits for evidence and then makes up her mind regarding what to do next. Typically, the lawyer argues that the evidence is not sufficient to prove guilt because presented evidence does not document in an adequate and convincing manner that the client has committed a crime. The lawyer may argue that the evidence only proves misconduct that cannot lead to a prison sentence for the client. Uncertainty and doubt should benefit the client, every defense lawyer will argue. It is every defense lawyer's job to interpret laws and verdicts in a way that should lead to a not-guilty verdict for the client in court. This defense strategy is called substance defense. The attorney contributes substance to a case for the court.

White-collar crime lawyers also contribute substance defense like street-crime lawyers, but there are several differences, related both to points in time and to magnitude of contribution. A white-collar substance defense starts much earlier in the investigative process, and it may last much longer into all kinds of appeals and retrials. The magnitude of contribution is related to the level of detail and the scope of evidence. Often, financial crime is documented in details such as a single bank transaction, a single invoice, or a single stock trade carried out by a third person. The scope of evidence is often such that a lot of redundant and irrelevant material is presented to make sure that nothing is overlooked. Instead of waiting for the criminal case to be opened in court, the attorney starts substance defense as early as possible to potentially stop the case and the client from ever appearing in court. It is more the rule than exception that the defense lawyer, in fear of future consequences, is actively on the case already when there are merely suspicion and rumors circulating. More rumors and accusations within the organization, the police, and the public can in fact be helpful to the attorney, as the attorney may argue that the case should be more focused. For example, in a fraud case in Norway, a family was accused of insider trading. The case was heavily covered by the national media. The family owned a large Norwegian manufacturing company, but there were other shareholders as well. Initially in the case, both the father and mother as well as the daughter and son were investigated by the police. A defense lawyer for the daughter successfully helped to keep her out of the case, arguing that the police should be more focused. Despite the fact that the police found an SMS message on her phone saying "Pappa," which obviously means father, police detectives accepted her explanation that she called many persons her "Pappa," and the prosecution dismissed her case and never prosecuted her in court. The same thing happened to the mother. Only the father and son were prosecuted, and they were convicted to long prison sentences in court. Both have appealed their sentences, which will be reviewed by the higher courts.

In another book in the Yale Series, Weisburd et al. (1991) formulate how the white-collar defense lawyer is involved at a very early stage:

> From the time there is even a hint that a possible white-collar crime is under investigation by legal authorities, individuals suspected of involvement often begin to retain attorneys and to prepare to defend themselves. Early legal strategies may include negotiations with the agencies involved, the seeking of civil or out-of-court resolution of the case, and the trading of information in return for favorable treatment from the prosecutor's office. Other strategies include defense efforts to limit the scope of the information sought through subpoenaed documents and to curtail the information obtained by the government through search warrants and electronic surveillance (99).

Bjørn Stordrange, a well-known white-collar lawyer in Norway, defended Acta entrepreneur Fred Anton Ingebrigtsen, who was suspected of insider trading in the Acta stock. Early on, Stordrange expressed in public his frustration with several delays in police investigations (Haakaas, 2009):

> When the charge was out last summer, we were told that the investigation would be completed last fall. The time limit was changed to Easter and then again to October this year. Now we are told that it might be completed by Christmas (2).

Stordrange's many appearances in the media indicated both active substance defense in the Acta case and symbolic defense, which will be discussed later in this chapter. Stordrange was extremely proactive in terms of an organized crime suspicion, where the police wanted to use the Norwegian mafia rule on the case. Stordrange succeeded in convincing the police to drop the organized crime charge against Ingebrigtsen and his crime associates.

In Norway, white-collar attorneys are typically trying to influence police investigations at Økokrim. Økokrim is the main source of specialist skills for the police and prosecution authorities in their combat against financial and environmental crime (www.okokrim.no). Økokrim is similar to the Serious Fraud Office in the UK. SFO is an independent government department, operating under the superintendence of the Attorney General. Its purpose is to protect society by investigating and, if appropriate, prosecuting those who commit serious or complex fraud, bribery, and corruption and pursuing them and others to recover the proceeds of their crime. For example on March 11, 2013, SFO charged three men in a Ponzi-style scheme, and the men appeared at City of London Magistrates Court charged with conspiracy to defraud investors in an alleged investment fraud related to electrical contracts in the hotel sector (www.sfo.gov.uk).

There is currently a battle going on between defense attorneys and prosecutors in many white-collar crime cases related to the proceeds of financial crime. It should not be profitable to commit crime, and there should be no crime money waiting for the criminal when he leaves prison and is a free man again. Therefore, the prosecution works hard to collect and recover proceeds from crime. The attorney will argue that all the client wealth is from legal activities and should thus not be collected by the government. The prosecution will argue that most of the wealth is from criminal activities. In most jurisdictions, the prosecutor has to prove that the money stems from criminal activities. Some years ago in Norway, this was changed. Now the criminal has to prove, via the attorney, that wealth was created legally. If not, the money will be withdrawn from the criminal. Only what can be assessed as reasonable wealth if the criminal had stayed law-abiding all his life will the criminal be able to keep. Hence, the issue of proof has been moved from the prosecutor to the defense lawyer in Norway, where the defense lawyer has to work hard to make the client keep all his money, houses, boats, and cars. Therefore, the substance defense will focus on the successful business man who may have made a mistake, but who should keep all his wealth because it is based on hard (and law-abiding) work.

Information Control Strategy

Defense lawyers in white-collar crime cases tend to take charge of information control at an early stage. Instead of being at the receiving end of documents from the police and prosecution, the attorney is in a position where the flow of information can be monitored. Of particular interest to the attorney is crucial information that can harm the client's case. The flow of harmful facts, insights, and knowledge of causes and effects that might become legal evidence with the police is restricted and stopped by the lawyer. Know-what, know-how, and know-why that is damaging for the client is controlled by the lawyer.

Strategic substance defense is not necessarily the first defense strategy applied by the attorney in a white-collar case. The defense lawyer's very first goal can be to prevent the police from obtaining evidence that is harmful to the client and prevent that information being applied by police detectives to define and justify a formal charge for crime.

At this stage, it is not laws and verdicts that are of concern to the lawyer. All the lawyer is worried about is the flow of information that is transformed into evidence in police investigations. The attorney's job is all about preventing the police from acquiring evidence and making it difficult or even impossible for the police to understand pieces of information that they have obtained. It is all about stopping the investigation at an early stage so that the case is closed. This is the defense lawyer's information control strategy.

Information control implies that documents are kept hidden, and that clients and witnesses do not talk to investigators and other persons in public positions. It may also imply that individuals are protected from the press, so that only the lawyer makes statements about the case. Information control strategy is applied ahead of substance defense strategy whenever a white-collar crime case first is detected by the media, who then cause an initial police investigation. If the lawyer is successful in strategic information control, then raw material for legal argumentation is kept hidden from public attention and use. The case for prosecution is weakened because important pieces of information not known to the police are missing. The police do not know that information exists, and nobody is willing to tell them. If an investigation is considered a puzzle, where all pieces have to be in place to see the picture, then both missing pieces as well as ill-placed pieces will make it difficult to perceive, understand, and interpret the fragmented picture. Detectives may find themselves with a case that is impossible to solve and thus, decide to close it.

If the police are aware of information that they so far have not been able to collect, the defense lawyer may argue that the requested information is difficult to retrieve and irrelevant for the case. The lawyer may argue that the information is confidential, out of date, or linked to other problematic information. If the police have already collected the information, the defense lawyer may argue that the information cannot be applied in the specific case because authorities have obtained it in an unethical or inadmissible way, such as torture or endless interrogation.

These arguments when performing information control are made in order to influence the counterpart, either by convincing police it is not a good idea to press for information or press charges or by obtaining a court ruling stating that information should not be made available or should even be returned to the client or the client's lawyer. Procedure rules that support information control are communicated from the defense to the prosecution. For example, the defense lawyer may argue that the law prohibits the search for or collection of specific documents. A prosecutor may argue that the law allows it, but nevertheless must consider whether it is worth the fight with the defense lawyer at this stage.

A special case of information control occurs when it is a lawyer who is investigated by the police for white-collar crime, such as theft of client money placed in clients' accounts with the law firm. Client accounts with Norwegian law firms are confidential and not accessible to law enforcement authorities because account information may reveal information that violates the attorney-client privilege. As mentioned earlier, the attorney-client privilege is one of the oldest privileges known to the common law in the US and also in Norway. The privilege ensures that a client may provide information to his or her attorney in confidence, with the knowledge that such information is protected, and neither the client nor the attorney may be forced to disclose the information that has been shared to their judicial adversaries (Kopon and Sungaila, 2012). This privilege includes information about money in bank accounts managed by the attorney.

John Christian Elden is a well-known white-collar lawyer in Norway who denies the police reading client mail or looking into client accounts. In 2011, the police accused two lawyers of white-collar crime and wanted to get insights into those lawyers' affairs. Elden reacted strongly, saying, "The police abuse lawyers who only try to do their job" (Kirkebøen, 2011: 7).

When there are obvious reasons to believe that lawyers are involved in crime, they cannot hide behind confidentiality fences, police argued (Kirkebøen). Elden agreed with this, but the court refused police appeal for information access because the judge agreed with Elden that the two lawyers could not be suspected of crime directly linked to their profession as lawyers. Elden argued that the police were hunting lawyers that only tried to do their job defending their clients (Jonassen, 2011). Elden was successful in his information control strategy here.

White-collar crime money is sometimes hidden in tax havens. Law firm Thommessen was asked by police to reveal individuals behind large sums of money transferred to tax havens via Thommessen accounts. Thommessen denied doing it, and the Supreme Court of Norway voted in favor of Thommessen due to the attorney-client privilege: financial transactions are considered information that lawyers must keep confidential. Similarly, when tax authorities ask for access to account information they are denied access for the same reasons (Reiss-Andersen, 2011). Law firm Thommessen was successful with their information control strategy in this case.

Strategic information control can be applied by stopping or limiting the flow of information from the client to law enforcement agencies, by preventing the police from exploring and exploiting various sources for information collection, or by requesting the return of documents not used by police (Mann, 1985). "The defense attorney's aim is to instruct the client or third party holding inculpatory information how to refrain from disclosing it to the government and, if necessary, to persuade or force him to refrain" (7).

Inculpatory, also called "incriminating," information is that which shows that a person has been involved in a criminal act. It is self-revealing information by the suspect. Inculpatory information may be applied by law enforcement agencies as evidence to prove guilt. *Exculpatory* information helps prove that a person has not been involved in a criminal act. In the information control strategy, the defense lawyer attempts to stimulate the flow of exculpatory information and prevent the flow of inculpatory information.

A defense attorney's active information control strategy is normally kept secret to other parties in the case, including the client. Success is often dependent upon the lack of awareness among other parties, including the press.

When an attorney advises a client not to answer certain questions in the next interrogation and instead answer that he does not know or that he will have to check accounting first, the client is subject to information control. The attorney is applying the information control strategy via the client. The police know nothing about it. One result might be that the investigation is delayed or even terminated.

A well-known defense lawyer as well as judge in Norway, Langbach phrased the question of whether it is unethical to try to delay a case in his 1996 book, *Forsvareren (The Defense Lawyer)*:

> From the perspective of a defense lawyer, it is natural to have the view that it is the task of the prosecution to bring a case to court. If it is beneficial to the client to delay the case, and if delay can be caused by legal means, then it is ethically acceptable to do so. It is the task of the prosecution and the court to react to initiatives from the defense lawyer, and make sure progress occurs in the case. If the main goal of delaying a case is to make the case itself obsolete, then the lawyer has to consider his own reputation, when it becomes publicly known that he is an expert in delaying client criminal cases (134).

One reason to delay the case might be to make it obsolete after a number of years. Another reason might be to reduce the prison sentence as a consequence of late court proceedings (Langbach, 1996).

A former police officer, now academic at a university in the UK, expressed following opinions about white-collar crime lawyers in a personal e-mail to the author of this book in 2013:

> As an ex-police officer I anecdotally know that solicitors lie and use all forms of diabolical half-truths to get clients off. They are entrepreneurial in their use of knowledge and of systems to get results. Similar to detectives as entrepreneurs, they are continually working, lurking, and getting results.

Information control does not only occur in white-collar crime cases. In many other criminal cases, the attorney works to exclude pieces of evidence from law enforcement access and application. The attorney may argue that information is obtained by law enforcement in an illegal manner or that information is misleading or irrelevant to the case. What makes white-collar cases so special is that strategic information control is of key importance—it is sometimes the most important activity—to successfully defend a client. In other kinds of cases, information control is mainly a tactical maneuver to detract attention or delay the case temporarily.

Information control strategy is supported by the attorney-client privilege as well as the work-product privilege. While the attorney-client privilege shields any information communicated to an attorney, the work-product privilege protects information that can fairly be said to have been prepared or obtained because of the prospect of litigation (Oh, 2004).

Controlling Information Sources

Strategic information control is concerned with the flow of damaging information about the client. A defense attorney will attempt to prevent police from exploring and exploiting various sources of information collection. Strategic information control implies taking control over information sources that are most likely to be contacted by the police. The police have many information sources when they investigate a case, and these sources can, to a varying extent, be influenced by a defense attorney.

In intelligence work pertaining to investigating and preventing white-collar crime, a variety of information sources are available. Sheptycki (2007) lists the following information sources in policing for general corporate social responsibility work: victim reports, witness reports, police reports, crime scene examinations, historical data such as criminal records held by police agencies, prisoner debriefings, technical or human surveillance products, suspicious financial transactions reporting, and reports emanating from undercover police operations. Similarly, internal investigation units in business organizations can apply intelligence sources. Intelligence analysis may also refer to the records of other governmental departments and agencies, and other more open sources of information may also be used in elaborate intelligence assessment. Most of the information used to prevent and investigate financial crime is sensitive, complex, and the result of a time-consuming process.

However, Sheptycki found that most crime analysis is organized around existing investigation and prevention sector data. Intelligence analysis is typically framed in terms of pre-existing institutional ways of thinking. He argues that organized crime notification, classification, and measurement schemes tend to reify pre-existing notions of traditional policing practice.

According to this perspective, the defense lawyer will try to control all information sources available to detectives in general and strategic criminal analysts in particular. *Control* means to prevent the police from obtaining unfavorable information and help the police obtain information in favor of the client. Here are some of the information sources that the defense attorney will try to influence:

1. *Interview*. By means of interrogation of witnesses, suspects, reference persons, and experts, information is collected on crimes, criminals, times and places, organizations, criminal projects, activities, roles, etc.
2. *Network*. By means of informants in the criminal underworld as well as in legal businesses, information is collected on actors, plans, competitors, markets, customers, etc. Informants often have connections with persons that an investigating colleague would be unable to formally approach.
3. *Location*. By analyzing potential and actual crime scenes, information is collected on criminal procedures, criminal objects, crime evolution, etc. Hot spots for criminal activities and traces of crime can be found. Secret ransacking of suspicious places is one aspect of this information source. Crime scene photographs are important information elements.
4. *Documents*. Studying documents obtained through confiscation may provide information on ownership, transactions, accounts, etc. One such example is forensic accounting, which is the application of accounting tasks for an evidentiary purpose. Forensic accounting is the action of identifying, recording, settling, extracting, sorting, reporting, and verifying past financial data or other accounting activities for settling current or prospective legal disputes, or using such past financial data to project future financial data in order to settle legal disputes.
5. *Observation*. By means of anonymous personal presence, both individuals and activities can be observed. Both in the physical and the virtual world, observation is important in financial crime intelligence. An example is digital forensics, the art and science of applying computer science to aid the legal process. Successful cybercrime intelligence requires computer skills and modern systems in policing. It amounts to more than the technological, systematic inspection of electronic systems and their contents for evidence or supportive evidence of a criminal act; it also requires specialized expertise and tools when applied to intelligence in important areas such as the online victimization of children.

6. *Action.* Provocation and actions conducted by the investigating unit to cause reactions that yield intelligence information are at the heart of the action category. Undercover operations by police officers also belong to the action category.
7. *Surveillance.* Observation by means of video cameras and microphones belong to this information source. Many business organizations have surveillance cameras on their premises to control entrances and other critical areas. It is possible for the police to listen in on discussions in a room without the participants knowing. Harfield (2008: 64) argues that when surveillance is employed to produce evidence, the product is often considered incontrovertible; hence defense lawyers' focus on process rather than product when cross-examining surveillance officers: "An essentially covert activity, by definition surveillance lacks transparency and is therefore vulnerable to abuse by over-zealous investigators."
8. *Communication control.* Wiretapping in terms of interception belongs to this information source. Police listen in on what is discussed on a telephone or transmitted via a data line without the participants being aware. In the UK, the interception of communications (telephone calls, emails, letters, etc.) while generating intelligence to identify more conventional evidential opportunities is excluded from trial evidence by law—to the evident incredulity of law enforcement colleagues in other countries.
9. *Physical material.* This is the investigation of material in order to identify, for example, fingerprints on doors or bags or material to investigate blood splatters and identify blood type. Another example is legal visitation, which is an approach used to identify illegal material. Police search is another approach to physical material collection. DNA is emerging as an important information source and is derived from physical material such as hair or saliva.
10. *Internet.* As an open source, the Internet is an important tool in corporate crime intelligence for finding sources of general information and specific happenings. It is important to note that use of open sources is by no means a new activity, nor is it a new phenomenon of the Internet. Also, there are risks of using open sources such as self-corroboration.
11. *Policing systems.* Police records are readily available in most police agencies. For example, DNA records may prove helpful

when DNA material from new suspects is collected. Similarly, corporate social responsibility units may collate and develop records that do not violate privacy rights.
12. *employees.* Information from the local community is often supplied in the form of tips to local police, using law enforcement tip lines. Similarly, a corporate social responsibility unit can receive tips from employees in various departments.
13. *Accusations.* Victimized persons or organizations file claims with the appropriate law enforcement unit.
14. *Exchange.* International policing cooperation includes exchange of intelligence information. International partners for national police include national police in other countries as well as multinational organizations such as Europol and Interpol. Similarly, trade organizations and other entities for business organizations create exchanges for financial crime intelligence.
15. *Media.* Intelligence officers are exposed to the *news* by reading newspapers and watching TV.
16. *Control authorities.* Cartel agencies, stock exchanges, tax authorities, and other control authorities are suppliers of information to the corporate executives in the event of suspicious transactions.
17. *External data storage.* A number of business and government organizations store information that may prove useful in financial crime intelligence. For example, telecom firms store data about traffic in which both the sender and the recipient are registered with date and time of communication.

All these information sources have different characteristics. For example, information sources can be distinguished in terms of the extent of trustworthiness and accessibility.

Prisons and other correctional environments are potential places for several information sources and production of intelligence useful to law enforcement. The total prison environment, including the physical plant, the schedule regimens of both staff and inmates, and all points of ingress and egress, can be legitimately tapped for intelligence purposes in countries such as the United States. Since members of organized crime syndicates are often sophisticated in terms of using, or exploiting, the corrections environment to their advantage, police and corrections personnel need to be immersed in the intelligence operations and strategies of their respective agencies. Legal visitation and escape attempts are sources of information. Prisoners are reluctant to testify, and their credibility is easily attacked. Communication control is derived from inmate use of phones, visits, mail, and other contacts.

The 17 information sources can be classified into two main categories. The first category includes all person-oriented information sources, where the challenge in corporate intelligence is communication with individuals. The second category includes all media-oriented information sources, where the challenge in corporate intelligence is the management and use of different technological and other media. This distinction into two main categories leads to the following classification of 17 information sources:

A. Person-oriented information sources
   1. Interrogation in interview
   2. Informants in network
   5. Anonymous, individual presence undercover for observation
   6. Provocation through action
   12. Tips from citizens in local community
   13. Claims in accusations
   14. Information exchange in interorganizational cooperation

B. Media-oriented information sources
   3. Crime scenes at location
   4. Confiscated documents
   7. Video cameras for surveillance
   8. Interception for communication control
   9. Physical materials such as fingerprints
   10. Open sources such as Internet
   11. Internal records in policing systems
   15. News in the media
   16. Supply of information from control authorities
   17. External data storage

Combinations of information sources are selected in investigation and intelligence according to the crime under investigation. When forensic accounting is applied as document study, it is typically combined with interviews and observations, thereby integrating behavioral aspects into forensic accounting.

For defense lawyers, the approach to controlling information and their sources is dependent on whether information is mainly available from talking to people (such as in interviews), visiting places (such as hot spots), searching in archives (such as documents), or using information technology to collect and analyze data. The defense lawyer can play an active role in interviews by helping the suspect on a continuous basis in his explanation. While a detective may have one interpretation, findings at places can be interpreted quite differently by the defense lawyer. Access to archives can be limited by court order. Technological access can be limited both in terms of software available as well as denied access to data warehouses and databases.

Controlling Information Benefits

Information is the raw material in all police work. The relative importance of and benefits from pieces of information are dependent on the relevance to a specific crime case, the quality of information, and the timeliness of information. Information value in police work is determined by information adaptability to police tasks in an investigation. A smart defense lawyer can reduce information value, information quality, information security, legal and ethical compliance, information resources, as well as information requirements in law enforcement.

Chaffey and White (2011) distinguish between the following six information management themes:

1. *Information value* representing importance. Information can be prioritized in importance and better-quality sources identified so that improved information is delivered. Information value can be assessed in terms of its fitness for policing purpose. Once information has been identified as valuable, plans can then be put in place to protect it from deletion or modification, share it within a defined audience, and improve its quality. Lower-value information can either be improved to increase its relevance to police officers or removed from detailed reports to produce summaries.
2. *Information quality* in terms of content, time and form. The content dimension is concerned with accuracy (correct information), relevance (information can support decision making), completeness (no data items missing), conciseness (information is not too detailed), and scope (may be broad or narrow, internal or external to the organization). The time dimension is concerned with timeliness (available when needed—immediate or real-time information is a common requirement), currency (information is up to date), frequency (information supplied at

appropriate regular intervals), and time period (a time series covers the right period of time). The form dimension is concerned with clarity (information readily interpreted), detail (both summary "dashboard" views and detailed "drill-down" views may be required), order (data sorted in a logical order and can be modified), presentation (tabulations and graphs), and media (hard copy from printouts and soft copy electronically stored and displayed).

3. *Information security* to safeguard from accidental and deliberate modification or deletion by people and events. Information and the media on which it is held may be destroyed by security breaches. Information security refers to protection of information and the systems and hardware that use, store, and transmit that information. The key features of information security are availability (only to those eligible), confidentiality (only to those eligible), and authenticity and integrity (safeguarding accuracy of information).

4. *Legal and ethical compliance* to handle sensitivity. Information is held about individuals on computer systems. Governments have developed many laws both to protect individuals and to give government agencies access to information that may be needed for law enforcement.

5. *Information resource* for knowledge management. The police are collections of individuals that possess knowledge. Information becomes knowledge when it is interpreted by individuals and put into context. Knowledge is information combined with reflection, interpretation, and context, where skills and opinions are added to make sense to new insights. Knowledge becomes information when it is codified and stored in information systems.

6. *Information requirement* to technology. Information is handled electronically by computer systems. Technology support to achieve the objectives of the information management strategy involves selecting relevant information systems applications and infrastructure.

A defense lawyer can reduce information benefits by lowering its fitness for policing purposes. Information quality can be reduced in terms of accuracy, relevance, completeness, conciseness, and lack of scope. Information security can be violated by modification or deletion of information elements. Lack of legal and ethical compliance can be stressed by pinpointing incidents of information leakage from the police in the past. Information as a resource is harmed by making it more difficult for the police to make new insights. Finally, information can be passed on to the police in a format not suited for computer systems.

Controlling Third-Party Information

Mann (1985) emphasizes the difficulties of controlling information held by third parties. It is common knowledge among defense attorneys that many persons give information to the government, even after an investigation is underway. Controlling information held by third parties has the same goal as all other information control activities—keeping incriminating information from reaching the government. But the means must be adapted because the source of information, whether a person or a document, is not directly controlled or possessed by the client. Mann distinguishes between friends and enemies as third parties:

> Third parties holding inculpatory information may be friends or associates of the client, who are willing to cooperate if they are located in time and proper requests are made. Or they may be persons with directly adverse interests, who perhaps are loyal to government interests or who have other reasons for wanting to provide information to the government that inculpates another person (157).

Several strategies are used by attorneys to attempt to control the statements made and documents held by third parties. The defense attorney may use the client's power and influence to control third-party interactions with government agents, or the lawyer may try to influence third parties through representation of multiple clients, or through other lawyers.

If a third-party is perceived as an uncooperative enemy, it is typically a person who is openly hostile to the client. The hostile third-party can refuse to meet with the defense attorney, provide partial and misleading statements, and make outright and sometimes false accusations. According to Mann, it is as important for the defense attorney to interview hostile informants as friendly informants. With a properly aggressive approach, the hostile informant can often be drawn into an interview and caught in a contradiction, or he can change his story, provide exculpatory information unknowingly, or otherwise supply material that the attorney can use to impeach his credibility.

Symbolic Defense Strategy

A symbol is an object or phrase that represents an idea, belief, or action. Symbols take the form of words, sounds, gestures, or visual images. Symbolic defense is concerned with activities that represent defense, but in themselves are no defense. It is an alternative and a supplement to substance defense. Substance and symbolic defense are different arenas where the white-collar attorney can work actively to try to make the police close the case, to make the court dismiss the case, and to enable reopening of a case to enable the client to plead not guilty.

The purpose of symbolic defense is to communicate information and legal opinions by means of symbols. Examples of attorney opinions are concerns about unacceptable delays in police investigations, low-quality police work, or other issues related to police and prosecution work. Complaining about delays in police investigations is not substance defense, as the complaint is not expressing a meaning about the crime and possible punishment. Complaining is symbolic defense, where the goal is to mobilize sympathy for the white-collar client.

As defense lawyer for white-collar criminal Kjell Gunnar Finstad in the Norex Group, attorney Bjørn Stordrange was upset about the elapsed time of police investigation (Vanvik, 2010):

> It doesn't matter what explanation the police [have] to give. Time speaks for itself and this case, both in terms of evidence and in terms of the law. If this case had been presented in court five years ago, it might have been another issue. But now, witnesses in the case hardly remember what happened anymore. We find it quite surprising that the police now spend so many resources on a case that is mainly history (14).

The defense lawyer may use noise as strategy to distract from the core of the criminal case, argued state prosecutor Harald L. Grønlien in a comment to Stordrange in the same newspaper (Ravn and Schultz, 2011):

> Some defense lawyers have a strategy to make noise and divert attention away from the core of the case. Therefore, they bring in as many formalities to a case as possible, to cause derailing says Grønlien (13).

In the Transocean case, several attorneys were active in symbolic defense. One example is the protests against staff on the prosecution side, which included experienced lawyers from the law firm Schjødt. It was argued that the experienced defense lawyers could not work for the other side in this case, because some other lawyers in the Schjødt firm had been briefly involved with one of the prosecuted white-collar criminals years before. This issue became a court case in itself, ending up in the Norwegian Supreme Court, thereby delaying the Transocean court case start. The Supreme Court decided that the two lawyers from Schjødt could indeed work for the prosecution in the Transocean case.

However, the symbolic defense did not end with the negative Supreme Court decision. One of the prosecuted advisors in the Transocean case, Sverre E. Koch, lawyer and partner at the law firm Thommessen, went on to the association of attorneys, where he complained about Schjødt lawyers on the prosecution side. The association concluded that it was harmful to the integrity of these lawyers, and formally critiqued the Schjødt lawyers for their behavior (Grini, 2013). Nevertheless, the two lawyers from Schjødt ended up working on the prosecution side in the Transocean case.

Another example of symbolic defense in the Transocean case was the attorneys' concern with PowerPoint slides used by the prosecution in court. At the bottom of each slide it said, "Økokrim protects values." Økokrim is the Norwegian national authority for investigation and prosecution of economic crime. Defense attorneys argued that that the text was misleading and could influence court members. The attorneys did not try to suppress the text; they only expressed their criticism of the prosecution in the media, thereby creating more noise around the court case.

A third and final example of symbolic defense in the Transocean case was a link in the media between the tax fraud case in court and a media story about theft of Transocean tax documents from tax authority offices. The media story linked the theft incident directly to the court case. However, it could not be proven that there was a link. One of the defense attorneys in court, Reiss-Andersen (2012), became active in expressing criticism of the newspaper *Dagens Næringsliv (The Norwegian Business Daily)*, which brought the story.

It is not necessarily the white-collar attorney who contacts the media to conduct symbolic defense. One of the characteristics of a white-collar criminal is media interest in the person and the case, because the person has a position in society that was abused in financial crime. Now that the person is prosecuted in court, it is indeed interesting for the press and other media to tell the story to its audience. A media storm can lead to different results. One outcome might be that the offender, after a while, is perceived as a victim. Another outcome might be that the judge feels pressured to convict the person, because the public expects a tough sentence to be passed.

A judge may feel the pressure to convict a white-collar crime suspect. This is confirmed in an interview of a judge carried out by Wheeler et al. (1988):

> The more public awareness, the more public knowledge, the more media coverage a case receives, the more I'm likely to feel that a prison sentence is going to have a deterrent effect on others. I suppose this makes it more likely (for a white-collar offender) to get a prison sentence for the same act than a person who is not in the public eye (136).

Norwegian judge Langbach (1996) discusses whether a court is influenced by media coverage:

> It might be argued that courts are not influenced by media coverage. This is probably true for most professional judges. But others may be influenced, such as amateur judges and the police, although they also will claim that they remain objective in a case. However, there are high-profile cases where it is impossible not to get influenced by the media. For example, the prosecution may feel they have no other choice but to go to court with a high-profile case, even if they do not have the best of evidence for conviction (57).

White-collar crime attorneys vary in the extent to which they find media coverage a suitable option for symbolic defense. Ideally, each attorney should only have what is best for the client in mind. However, some famous attorneys may have their own media agenda, more or less independent of the current clients that they are defending in court. Irrespective of client and/or lawyer agenda, the lawyer must be prepared to respond to media inquiries. The client may want to present the story in the press because he or she may believe that press coverage will have a positive impact on personal image as well as court proceedings. Police statements in the press may be perceived as provocation against the client, who wants to tell another story.

Symbolic defense strategy can also be applied between rounds in court. Maybe the case is completed in a district court and is waiting in line for a court of appeals. Often, it takes several months, sometimes a year, to start court proceedings in courts of appeals and finally in the Supreme Court. While waiting for proceedings to start in a higher court, a defense lawyer may find it adequate to continue defense activities. An example is well-known attorney Stordrange, who argued that the prosecution document in the Acta case of insider trading was not according to required standards. Specifically, Stordrange argued that a prosecution document should list each and every transaction where there is suspicion of insider trading, rather than just a sum of transactions (Ånestad, 2013):

> "If the court finds it missing, then parts of the prosecution document need to be rewritten, and the district court sentence has to be lifted," says Bjørn Stordrange, who is defense lawyer for Acta entrepreneur Fred A. Ingebrigtsen (9).

Here we find a defense strategy of trying to cancel the sentence from district court, where the client Fred A. Ingebrigtsen was sentenced to nine years in prison for insider trading in Acta stocks. This sentence is the most severe verdict ever passed in a Norwegian court for financial crime.

4

Lawyers as Knowledge Workers

A law firm is generally composed of lawyers, paralegals, managers, support personnel, and administrators. Most law firms use a partnership form of organization. In such a framework, lawyers who are highly effective in using and applying knowledge in fee earnings are eventually rewarded with partner status and thus own stakes in the firm. These diverse occupations have distinct functions, yet these individuals must work together to achieve the desired outcome of adding value to the firm. Lawyers represent their clients in legal matters by presenting evidence and legal arguments and provide counsel to clients concerning their legal rights and obligations.

Lawyers are competent in general legal principles and procedures and in the substantive and procedural aspects of the law, and they have the ability to analyze and provide solutions to legal problems. Lawyers are knowledge workers. They are professionals who have gained knowledge through formal education (explicit) and through learning on the job (tacit). After completing their advanced educational requirements, most law students enter their careers as associates in law. In this role, they continue to learn and, thus, they gain significant tacit knowledge through learning by doing.

Senior fee earners care more for the overall success of the firm, either because they are partners or because they are senior associates responsible for driving business to the firm. They see the benefit of knowledge management (KM) when they can task more junior fee earners on matters, and the senior fee earners can do the job more quickly, or because they themselves use the know-how systems more and understand the necessity for KM. Senior fee earners have had more contact with KM as they have been around the firm longer and found it valuable. In order to earn higher fees, they need to be more efficient and therefore tap into reusable know-how more frequently.

Characteristics of Knowledge

There are many definitions of knowledge. Some describe it as justified true belief. Definitions of organizational knowledge range from a complex, accumulated expertise that resides in individuals and is partly or largely inexpressible to a much more structured and explicit content. There are also several classifications of knowledge—implicit explicit, embodied, encoded, embedded, event, procedural, and common are just a few examples. Knowledge has long been recognized as a valuable resource for the organizational growth and sustained competitive advantage, especially for organizations competing in uncertain environments. Recently, some researchers have argued that knowledge is an organization's most valuable resource because it represents intangible assets, operational routines, and creative processes that are hard to imitate. However, the effective management of knowledge is fundamental to the organization's ability to create and sustain competitive advantage.

Knowledge is a renewable, reusable, and accumulating resource of value to the organization when applied in the production of products and services. Knowledge cannot as such be stored in computers; it can only be stored in the human brain. Knowledge is what a knower knows; there is no knowledge without someone knowing it. The perspective of knowledge applied in this book is derived from the resource-based theory of the firm. Knowledge that is valuable, unique, difficult to imitate, combinable, difficult to substitute and exploitable can provide the basis for firms' competitive advantages.

The need for a knower in knowledge existence raises the question as to how knowledge can exist outside the heads of individuals. Although knowledge cannot *originate* outside the heads of individuals, it can be argued that knowledge can be represented by and often embedded in organizational processes, routines, and networks, and sometimes in document repositories. However, knowledge is seldom complete outside of an individual.

In this book, knowledge is defined as information combined with experience, context, interpretation, reflection, intuition, and creativity. Information becomes knowledge once it is processed in the mind of an individual. This knowledge then becomes information again once it is articulated or communicated to others in the form of text, computer output, spoken or written words, or other means. Six characteristics of knowledge can distinguish it from information: knowledge is a human act, knowledge is the residue of thinking, knowledge is created in the present moment, knowledge belongs to communities, knowledge circulates through communities in many ways, and new knowledge is created at the boundaries of old. A pragmatic definition defines knowledge as the most valuable form of content in a continuum starting at data, encompassing information, and ending at knowledge.

Typically, data is classified, summarized, transferred, or corrected in order to add value and become information within a certain context. This conversion is relatively mechanical and has long been facilitated by storage, processing, and communication technologies. These technologies add place, time, and form utility to the data. In doing so, the information serves to inform or reduce uncertainty within the problem domain. Therefore, information is united with the context, that is, it only has utility within the context.

Knowledge has the highest value, the most human contribution, the greatest relevance to decisions and actions, and the greatest dependence on a specific situation or context. It is also the most difficult content type to manage, because it originates and is applied in the minds of human beings. People who are knowledgeable not only have information, but also have the ability to integrate and frame the information within the context of their experience, expertise, and judgment. In doing so, they can create new information that expands the state of possibilities and, in turn, allows for further interaction with experience, expertise, and judgment. Therefore, in an organizational context, all new knowledge stems from people. Some knowledge is incorporated in organizational artifacts like processes, structures, and technology. However, institutionalized knowledge often inhibits competition in a dynamic context, unless adaptability of people and processes (higher order learning) is built into the institutional mechanisms themselves.

Our concern with distinctions between information and knowledge is based on real differences as well as technology implications. Real differences between information and knowledge do exist, although for most practical purposes these differences are of no interest at all. Information technology implications are concerned with the argument that computers can only manipulate electronic information, not electronic knowledge. Business systems are loaded with information, but they have no knowledge.

Some have defined knowledge as a fluid mix of framed experience, values, contextual information, and expert insights that provides a framework for evaluating and incorporating new experiences and information. It originates and is applied in the mind of a knower. In organizations, it often becomes embedded not only in documents or repositories but also in organizational routines, processes, practices, and norms.

Explicit Knowledge and Tacit Knowledge

A distinction can be made between explicit and tacit knowledge. Explicit knowledge is easily expressed in words and numbers and shared in forms such as data, scientific formulae, specifications, manuals, documents, artifacts, and computers and is collectively distributed and scattered in different locations and embedded in documents and other forms, both electronically and on paper It is relatively simple to share this kind of knowledge in law firms. During in-company training for example, explicit knowledge is shared among lawyers. Explicit knowledge in law firms can be expressed in legal concepts and shared in the form of legal manuals, and the like.

Tacit knowledge, on the other hand, is highly personal and hard to formalize, making it difficult to communicate or share with others. Subjective insights, intuitions, and hunches are examples of this kind of knowledge. Tacit knowledge is deeply rooted in an individual's actions and experience as well as in the ideals, values, or emotions that person embraces. The extent to which knowledge is tacit may be considered a variable, with the degree of tacit characteristics being a function of the extent to which the knowledge is or can be codified and abstracted, communicated and embedded in information documents.

Tacit knowledge may exist individually in the human mind and experience and in a person's know-what, know-how, know-why or collectively in the form of codified routines and in-house processes or embedded in the social context of a law firm. The concept of tacit knowledge corresponds closely to the concept of knowledge with a low level of codification. Codification is the degree to which the knowledge is fully documented or expressed in writing at the time of transfer between two persons. The complexity of knowledge increases with lower levels of codification. A similar distinction that scholars frequently make is between practical, experience-based knowledge and the theoretical knowledge derived from reflection and abstraction from that experience.

Examples of explicit legal knowledge include case law, legislation, precedents, best practice and model documents, business and industry information, checklists, methodologies, policies and procedures, financial information relating to cases and matters, standardized techniques of investigation, and previous case handling.

Examples of tacit legal knowledge include expertise of lawyers, client information, lessons learned from past matters and projects, tips at drafting pleadings or documents, leads from experts on a research topic, hints at arguing motions and applications, relationships and other social aspects that might influence case handling.

While we make a distinction between explicit and tacit knowledge here, the important thing is not a clear distinction, but rather our understanding of tacit extent, codification possibilities, and externalization. Knowledge may dynamically shift between tacit and explicit over time as knowledge is applied to legal problems. What is tacit now may become explicit the next time, and what is explicit now, may later return to the source as a new insight of tacit character.

From Information via Knowledge to Wisdom

Distinctions are often made between data, information, knowledge and wisdom. *Data* are letters and numbers without meaning. Data are independent, isolated measurements, characters, numerical characters, and symbols. Data refers to unstructured, objective facts, the noninterpreted signals that reach a person's senses every minute by the zillions. Typically, data is classified, summarized, transferred, or corrected in order to add value and become information within a certain context.

Information is data that is included in a context that makes sense. For example, "40 degrees" can have different meaning depending on the context. There can be a medical, geographical, or technical context. If a person has a 40-degree Celsius fever, that is quite serious. If a city is located 40 degrees north, we know that it is far south of Norway. If an angle is 40 degrees, we know what it looks like. Information is data that makes sense because it can be understood correctly. People turn data into information by organizing it into some unit of analysis, for example, dollars, dates, or customers. Information is data endowed with relevance and purpose. People attach meaning to data. Information serves to inform or reduce uncertainty within the problem domain. Therefore, information is united with the context; that is, it only has utility within the context.

Information becomes knowledge once it is processed in the mind of a person. This knowledge then becomes information again once it is articulated or communicated to colleagues or clients in the form of text, computer output, spoken or written words, or other means. The relation between data, information, and knowledge is recursive. Value is added to data, turning it into information. Information becomes knowledge when it is processed in the mind of an individual. This knowledge then moves down the value chain and becomes information. In a legal context, the provision of legal information is a service offered by legal information professionals and implies the provision of appropriate materials to legal practitioners.

Knowledge is information combined with experience, context, interpretation, and reflection. Knowledge is a renewable resource that accumulates in an organization through use and in combination with employees' experience. Humans have knowledge; knowledge cannot exist outside the heads of individuals in the company. Information becomes knowledge when it enters the human brain. This knowledge transforms back into information when it is articulated and communicated to others. Information is an explicit representation of knowledge; it is in itself *not* knowledge. Knowledge can both be truths and lies, perspectives and concepts, judgments and expectations. Knowledge is used to receive information by analyzing, understanding, and evaluating; by combining, prioritizing, and decision making; and by planning, implementing, and controlling. The relation between data, information, and knowledge is recursive. Value is added to data, turning it into information. Information becomes knowledge when it is processed in the mind of an individual. This knowledge then moves down the value chain and becomes information again.

Legal knowledge, knowledge of law and its application, is used to procure, produce, and manage legal work. Moreover, it is possessed by humans, agents, or other active entities. And last but not least, it is knowledge that has the ability to cause things to happen, as it is knowledge that causes individuals to act.

Knowledge can also be described as justified true belief. Definitions of organizational knowledge range from a complex, accumulated expertise that resides in individuals and is partly or largely inexpressible to a much more structured and explicit content. There are also several classifications of knowledge, such as explicit, embodied, encoded, embedded, event, procedural, and common.

Knowledge has long been recognized as a valuable resource for the organizational growth and sustained competitive advantage, especially for organizations competing in uncertain environments. Recently, some researchers have argued that knowledge is an organization's most valuable resource because it represents intangible assets, operational routines, and creative processes that are hard to imitate.

Knowledge is a renewable, re-usable, and accumulating asset of value to firms that increases in value with employee experience and organizational life. Knowledge is intangible, without boundaries, and dynamic, and if it is never used at a specific time in a specific place, it is of no value. Knowledge is what a knower knows; there is no knowledge without someone knowing it. Knowledge therefore must be viewed as originating "between the ears" of individuals. Taken literally, the need for a knower raises profound questions as to whether and how knowledge can exist outside the heads of individuals. Although knowledge can be represented in and often embedded in organizational processes, routines, and networks, and sometimes in document repositories, it cannot truly originate outside the mind. Nor is it ever complete outside of an individual. Knowledge is part of an organization's capital. The knowledge and knowing capability of an organization might also be referred to as "intellectual capital." This terminology has a clear parallel with the concept of human capital, which embraces the acquired knowledge, skills, and capabilities that enable persons to act in new ways.

Knowledge has the highest value, the most human contribution, the greatest relevance to decisions and actions, and the greatest dependence on a specific situation or context. It is also the most difficult of content types to manage, because it originates and is applied in the minds of human beings. People who are knowledgeable not only have information, but also have the ability to integrate and frame the information within the context of their experience, expertise, and judgment. In doing so, they can create new information that expands the state of possibilities and in turn allows for further interaction with experience, expertise, and judgment. Therefore, in an organizational context, all new knowledge stems from people. Some knowledge is incorporated in organizational artifacts like processes, structures, and technology.

However, institutionalized knowledge often inhibits competition in a dynamic context unless higher order learning is built into the institutional mechanisms themselves.

To understand the concept of legal knowledge is to distinguish between its acquisition, its entity, and its justification. Understanding, or acquiring, the content of a piece of knowledge can be achieved through different routes, for instance by using deductive, inductive, or mathematical reasoning. The second distinction is its entity. A piece of knowledge can be a purely legal entity, which is abstract (a general rule of law), or it can be concrete, as a concrete case description. Thirdly, justification of the content of a piece of knowledge can be attained through either the formal sources of law (case law and statutory law) or through the material sources of law (common law).

Knowledge can be viewed from different perspectives. From a personal perspective, knowledge is viewed as existing in the individual. From a social perspective, knowledge is created and inherent in the collective actions of a group of people working together and dependent on the social context where they belong. The organizational perspective draws from the data, information, and knowledge perspective. The social perspective utilizes a deeper understanding of knowledge formed through unique patterns of interactions between technologies, processes, techniques, and people, which is shaped by the organization's unique history and culture. The distinction between data, information and knowledge may lead to a distinction between data management, information management, and knowledge management. Compared to data and information management, knowledge management goes beyond the storage and manipulation of information and data: It has to do with human resources management.

Wisdom is knowledge combined with learning, insights, and judgmental abilities. Wisdom is more difficult to explain than knowledge, because the levels of context become even more personal. Thus the higher-level nature of wisdom renders it more obscure than knowledge. While knowledge is mainly sufficiently generalized solutions, wisdom is best thought of as sufficiently generalized approaches and values that can be applied in numerous and varied situations. Wisdom cannot be created like data and information, and it cannot be shared with others like knowledge. Because the context is so personal, it becomes almost exclusive to our own minds and incompatible with the minds of others without extensive transaction. This transaction requires not only a base of knowledge and opportunities for experiences that help create wisdom, but also the processes of introspection, retrospection, interpretation, and contemplation. We can value wisdom in others, but we can only create it ourselves.

It has been argued that expert systems using artificial intelligence are able to do knowledge work. The chess-playing computer called Deep Blue, created by IBM, is frequently cited as an example. Deep Blue can compete with the best human players because chess, though complex, is a closed system of unchanging rules that are codified. The size of the board never varies, the rules are unambiguous, the moves of the pieces are clearly defined, and there is absolute agreement about what it means to win or lose. Deep Blue is no knowledge worker; the computer only performs a series of computations at extremely high speed.

Some argue that knowledge can be managed, even if a very personal perspective of knowledge is assumed. They focus on organizing the law firm staff as inquirers by facilitating and creating an environment for those who engage in the act of seeking information for a purposeful objective.

From Core via Advanced to Innovative Knowledge

Distinctions can be made between core, advanced, and innovative knowledge. These knowledge categories indicate different levels of knowledge sophistication. Core knowledge is that minimum scope and level of knowledge required for daily operations, while advanced knowledge enables an organization to be competitively viable and innovative knowledge is the knowledge that enables the organization to lead its industry and competitors.

Core knowledge is the basic knowledge required to stay in business. This is the type of knowledge that can create efficiency barriers for entry of new companies, as new competitors are not up to speed in basic business processes. Since core knowledge is present at all existing competitors, the firm must have this knowledge even though it will provide the firm with no advantage that distinguishes it from its competitors. Core knowledge is that minimum scope and level of knowledge required to just play the game. Having that level of knowledge and capability will not assure the long-term competitive viability of the firm, but does present a basic industry knowledge to stay in business as long as the industry does not change. Basic knowledge is required for a lawyer, as knowledge worker, to understand and interpret information, and basic knowledge is required for a law firms, as knowledge organizations, to receive inputs and produce outputs. Core knowledge alone produces only elementary and basic results of little value and low quality. Core knowledge tends to be commonly held by members of an industry and therefore provides little advantage other than over nonmembers (Zack, 1999).

In a law firm, examples of core knowledge include knowledge of the law, knowledge of the courts, knowledge of clients, and knowledge of procedures. For a student in business school, core knowledge includes knowledge of what subjects to study this term and where the lectures take place.

Since core knowledge is expected of all competitors, you must have it even though it will provide your company with no advantage that distinguishes it from its competitors. Let us take two examples from the business world: One from the consumer electronics (hard product) business and one from Internet programming (soft product).

To enter the modem manufacturing market, a new company must have extensive knowledge of suitable circuit design, all electronic parts that go into a modem, fabricating surface mount (SMD) chip boards, how to write operating system drivers for modems, and familiarity with computer telephony standards. Similarly, a company developing websites for florists needs server hosting capabilities, Internet programming skills, graphic design skills, clearly identified target markets, and necessary software. In either case, just about any competitor in those businesses is assumed to have this knowledge in order to compete in their respective markets. Such essential knowledge, therefore, provides no advantage over other market players.

Advanced knowledge is what makes an organization competitively visible and active. Such knowledge allows the firm to differentiate its products and services from that of a competitor through the application of superior knowledge in certain areas. Such knowledge allows the firm to compete head-on with its competitors in the same market and for the same set of customers. Advanced knowledge enables a firm to be competitively viable. The firm may have generally the same level, scope, or quality of knowledge as its competitors, although the specific knowledge content will often vary among competitors, enabling knowledge differentiation. Firms may choose to compete on knowledge head-on in the same strategic position, hoping to know more than a competitor, or they instead may choose to compete for that position by differentiating their knowledge (Zack, 1999).

Advanced knowledge is knowledge necessary to get acceptable work done. Advanced knowledge is required for a lawyer as a knowledge worker to achieve satisfactory work performance, and advanced knowledge is required for a law firm as a knowledge organization to produce legal advice and legal documents that are acceptable to clients. When advanced knowledge is combined with basic knowledge, then we find professional knowledge workers and professional knowledge organizations in the legal industry.

In a law firm, examples of advanced knowledge include knowledge of law applications, knowledge of important court rulings, and knowledge of successful procedural case handling. For a student in the business school, advanced knowledge includes knowledge of important articles and books that are compulsory literature in subjects for the term.

Advanced knowledge is what makes your company competitively viable. Such knowledge allows your company to differentiate its product from that of a competitor, arguably, through the application of superior knowledge in certain areas. Such knowledge allows your company to compete head-on with its competitors in the same market and for the same set of customers. In the case of the company trying to compete in modem manufacturing markets, superior or user-friendly software or an additional capability in modems (such as warning online users of incoming telephone calls) represents such knowledge. In the case of the website development firm, such knowledge might be about international flower markets and collaborative relationships in Dutch flower auctions that the company can use to improve websites delivered to its customers.

Innovative knowledge allows a firm to lead its entire industry to an extent that clearly differentiates it from competition. Such knowledge allows a firm to change the rules of the game by introducing new business practices and to expand its market share by winning new customers and increasing service levels to existing customers. Innovative knowledge is that knowledge that enables a firm to lead its industry and competitors and to significantly differentiate itself from its competitors. Innovative knowledge often enables a firm to change the rules of the game (Zack, 1999).

Innovative knowledge is knowledge that makes a real difference. When lawyers in a firm apply innovative knowledge in analysis and reasoning based on incoming and available information, then new insights are generated in terms of situation patterns, actor profiles, and client strategies. When lawyers apply innovative knowledge, then new procedures and methods are introduced that create an advantage in the industry.

In a law firm, examples of innovative knowledge include knowledge of standardizing repetitive legal cases, knowledge of successful settlements, and knowledge of modern information technology to track and store vast amounts of information from various sources. For a student in the business school, innovative knowledge includes knowledge of important topics within subjects, links between subjects, typical exam questions, and knowledge of business cases where theory can be applied.

Patented technology is an applicable example of changing the rules. Patents cannot always protect innovative knowledge, as the lawsuit between Microsoft and Apple in the 1980s should serve to remind us. Apple sued Microsoft for copying the look and feel of its graphical user interface (GUI). The US Supreme Court ruled that things like look and feel could not be patented; they can only be copyrighted. Microsoft won the case, since it copied the look and feel but used entirely different code to create its product in the first place.

From Know-What via Know-How to Know-Why

Knowledge levels were here defined as basic knowledge, advanced knowledge, and innovative knowledge. An alternative approach is to define knowledge levels in terms of knowledge depth: know-what, know-how, and know-why respectively. These knowledge depth levels represent the extent of insight and understanding about a phenomenon. While know-what is simple perception of what is going on, know-why is complicated insight into cause-and-effect relationships about why things are going on.

Know-what is knowledge about what is happening. A lawyer perceives that something is going on that might need attention. The lawyer's insight is limited to perception of something happening. The lawyer understands neither how it is happening nor why it is happening.

Know-how is knowledge about how a legal case develops, how a criminal behaves, how investigations can be carried out, or how a criminal business enterprise is organized. The lawyer's insight is not limited to a perception of something is happening; he or she also understands how it is happening or how it is. Similarly, know-how is present when the lawyer understands how legal work is to be carried out and how the client will react to advice put forward in the process.

Know-why is the knowledge representing the deepest form of understanding and insights into a phenomenon. The lawyer and the members of the law firm do not only know that something occurs and how it occurs, they also have developed an understanding of why it occurs. They do not only know what is going on and how it is occurring, an understanding of causality is also present. Developing hypotheses about cause-and-effect relationships and empirically validating causality are important characteristics of know-why knowledge.

Declarative, Procedural, and Analytical Knowledge

In support of the law firm's KM objective and strategy, in general lawyers must manage the following types of knowledge: administrative data, declarative knowledge, procedural knowledge, and analytical knowledge.

Administrative data includes all of the nuts and bolts information about firm operations, such as hourly billing rates for lawyers, client names and matters, staff payroll data, and client invoice data.

Declarative knowledge (know-that and know-what) is "knowledge of the law," the legal principles contained in statutes, court opinions, and other sources of primary legal authority. Law students spend most of their law school careers acquiring this kind of knowledge. For practical reasons this type of knowledge and explicit knowledge may be treated as synonymous because declarative knowledge is knowledge that can be articulated.

Procedural knowledge (know-how) is knowledge of the mechanics of complying with the law's requirements in a particular situation—what documents are necessary to transfer an asset from company A to company B or what forms must be filed when creating a new corporation.

Analytical knowledge (know-why) is the sum of the conclusions reached about the course of action a particular client should follow in a particular situation. Analytical knowledge results from analyzing declarative knowledge (i.e., substantive law principles) as it applies to a particular fact setting.

These are knowledge categories of importance to all law firms. However, not all kinds of knowledge are crucial knowledge. To make the decision to invest in knowledge, it is very important for an organization to know what knowledge is relevant to the organization and what knowledge adds value. Crucial knowledge includes at least the ever-changing knowledge that is necessary to operate within the industry at an acceptable level. Crucial knowledge is often incorporated in the form of tacit knowledge that manifests itself as problem-solving behavior. The crucial aspect of knowledge is therefore primarily viewed as the availability of such problem-solving behaviors in the light of the continuity of the organization.

Core Competence and Capabilities

Core competencies are the collective learning in the organization, especially how the diverse service skills and multiple streams of technologies coordinate within the company. Since core competence is about harmonizing streams of technology, it is also about the organization of work and the delivery of value. Core competence does not diminish with use. Unlike physical assets, which do deteriorate over time, competencies are enhanced as they are applied and shared.

But competencies still need to be nurtured and protected; knowledge fades if it is not used. Competencies are the glue that binds existing business and coordinate service innovation. They are also the engines for new business development. At least three tests can be applied to identify core competencies in a company. First, a core competence provides potential access to a wide variety of markets. Second, a core competence should make a significant contribution to the perceived customer benefits of the end product. Finally, a core competence should be difficult for competitors to imitate.

A study investigated the competencies of lawyers in South African law firms (Du Plessis, 2008). Lawyers responding indicated that being a competent lawyer involves the following:

- knowing how to find appropriate information, 95 percent
- knowing where to find appropriate information, 95 percent
- providing timely and accurate information to relevant people, 92 percent
- developing a personal system for finding information, 65 percent
- oral communication skills, 46 percent
- written communication skills, 90 percent
- decision-making skills, 80 percent
- problem solving skills, 89 percent
- creative thinking skills, 67 percent
- presentation or public speaking skills, 30 percent

- building working relationships, 37 percent
- organizing and managing information resources, 72 percent
- keeping up with new information, 95 percent
- computer competency, 56 percent

The tangible link between identified core competencies and end products is called core products—the embodiments of one or more core competencies. Core products are the components or subassemblies that actually contribute to the value of the end products. Core competencies are sometimes called firm-specific competencies, resource deployments, invisible assets, and distinctive competencies.

Some argue that core competencies are not products or those things we do relatively well. Instead they are those activities, usually intellectually based service activities or systems, that the company performs better than any other enterprise and through which a company creates uniquely high value for customers. Developing best-in-the-world capabilities is crucial in designing a core competency strategy. Unless the company is best in the world at an activity it is someone else's core competency. The company gives up competitive edge by not buying that skill from a best-in-the-world source.

Competence and capability are terms often used interchangeably. However, competence represents implicit and invisible assets, while capability represents an explicit knowledge set. Some researchers adopt a knowledge-based view of the firm and define core capability as the knowledge set that distinguishes and provides competitive advantage. There are four dimensions to this knowledge set. Its content is embodied in (1) employee knowledge and skills and embedded in (2) technical systems. The processes of knowledge creation and control are guided by (3) managerial systems. The fourth dimension is (4) the values and norms associated with the various types of embodied and embedded knowledge and with the processes of knowledge creation and control.

Some researchers suggest that capabilities build on the notion of competencies but focus on the role of management in building and adapting these competencies to address rapidly changing environments. Dynamic capabilities help enterprises to identify opportunities and mobilize competencies by reallocating resources. The ability to adapt and extend existing competencies is a key characteristic of dynamic capabilities. This ability places responsibility for entrepreneurship on executive management, as they must be able to accurately sense changes and opportunities. They must also act on these opportunities to be able to seize them by reconfiguring both tangible and intangible assets to meet new challenges.

Similar to core competencies, capabilities are considered "core" if they differentiate a company strategically. The concept is not new. Their strategic significance has been discussed for decades, stimulated by the research discovery that of nine diversification strategies, the two that were built on an existing skill or resource base in the firm were associated with the highest performance. The observation that industry-specific capabilities increased the likelihood a firm could exploit a new technology within that industry has confirmed the early work.

Therefore some authors suggest that effective competition is based less on strategic leaps than on incremental innovation that exploits carefully developed capabilities. On the other hand, institutionalized capabilities may lead to incumbent inertia in the face of environmental changes. Technological discontinuities can enhance or destroy existing competencies within an industry. Such shifts in the external environment resonate within the organization, so that even seemingly minor innovations can undermine the usefulness of deeply embedded knowledge. All innovation necessarily requires some degree of creative destruction.

A capability is defined as dynamic if, in a rapidly changing environment, it enables the firm to modify itself so as to continue to produce, efficiently and/or effectively, market offerings for some market segments.

5

Law Firms as Knowledge Organizations

A new perspective on knowledge in organizations is being created. Organizations are viewed as bodies of knowledge, and knowledge management is considered an increasingly important source of competitive advantage for organizations. The special capabilities of organizations for creating and transferring knowledge are being identified as a central element of organizational advantage. Knowledge embedded in the organization's business processes and the employee's skills provide the firm with unique capabilities to give clients a product or service. Scholars and observers from disciplines as disparate as sociology, economics, and management science agree that a transformation has occurred—knowledge is at center stage.

Law firms have always been pure knowledge organizations, always conscious of the fact that their sustainable advantage is the expertise and knowledge of their lawyers, and their firms, rather than any physical factors of service production. The growing awareness of knowledge and its value in organizations from the last decade of the twentieth century, coupled with the changes in the business environment, has resulted in progressive law firms investigating alternative ways of providing cost-efficient structures and high-quality services that may sharpen their competitiveness and broaden their influence within the legal industry and the global economy.

The legal industry is faced with many changes in the business environment. Some of the major changes are mergers and acquisitions in the industry, new information technology for knowledge management, globalization of legal services, increased specialization in the practice of law, more knowledgeable and demanding clients, and increased profit-orientation among partners.

As law firms worldwide constantly strive for competitive advantage, major approaches and tools in pursuing their objectives are knowledge management (KM) and information technology (IT). The attention for a knowledge-based perspective on organizations has led to both scientific and practical interest in organizing firms with the help of knowledge management. The importance of knowledge to organizations has been extensively established in the business and management literature as being the basis of future sustainable competitive advantage. Knowledge is the stock-in-trade for law firms and other professional service firms.

Knowledge-Based View of the Firm

This book applies the knowledge-based view of the firm as its main theoretical perspective. The knowledge-based view is part of the resource-based view of the firm, which views the firm as a collection of productive resources. According to the resource-based theory of the firm, performance differences across firms can be attributed to the variance in the firms' resources and capabilities.

The essence of the resource-based theory of the firm lies in its emphasis on the internal resources available to the firm rather than on the external opportunities and threats dictated by industry conditions and market change. Knowledge is considered an important resource in most firms. The resource-based view of the firm posits that firm competitiveness comes from unique bundles of tangible and intangible assets that are valuable, rare, imperfectly imitable, irreplaceable, combinable, and sustainable.

The knowledge-based view considers knowledge as the critical input in production of legal services in the law firm. Knowledge is the primary source of value of the firm. Based on the assumption of bounded rationality, this view assumes that individuals will never possess identical stocks of knowledge. Since each firm has its unique set of human resources in terms of lawyers as knowledge workers, there will always be knowledge asymmetries between law firms (Dibbern et al., 2008).

Knowledge management (KM) is mainly introduced to help companies create, share, and use knowledge effectively. Organizational theorists have, for example, emphasized that information and knowledge acquired by one part of an organization must be communicated speedily to other parts. However, organization members collectively acquire enormous quantities of information on an ongoing basis; if all such information were to be transmitted to all parts of the organization, its members might simply suffer from information overload.

Methods for identification of information needs may be adopted from related areas, such as executive information systems where legal tasks define knowledge needs. Effective knowledge management pays off in fewer mistakes, less redundancy, quicker problem solving, improved decision making, reduced research development costs, increased worker independence, enhanced customer relations, improved service, and much more. Knowledge support functions have to be established to implement and continuously improve KM in an organization. Some knowledge organizations, such as law firms, have introduced the role of the Chief Knowledge Officer (CKO), which is not so much to provide KM facilities and services as to enable the organization to learn, to innovate, and to gain from entrepreneurship. The CKO has to discover and develop a law firm's implicit vision of how KM will make a difference for that particular organization.

The increased efforts in most law firms to improve their knowledge management are related to a number of changes in the legal industry (Susskind, 2010). First, there is a shift from paper-based to electronic documentation. Second, advances in information and communication technology enable storing, transfer, and exchange of information electronically as a supplement to meetings and phone calls. Electronic services available on the Internet make lawyers interact with a number of external service providers electronically, rather than interacting through internal functions. Globalization of legal services requires law firms locally to act globally for corporate clients that are doing business in several parts of the world.

The drive toward specialization needs to be combined with generalization, where specialists share their understanding with other specialists as well as clients. Merging expertise advice and sometimes translating it into something understandable for the layman is enabled in KM by putting together electronic pieces of text, images, videos, and soundtracks.

Knowledge management is not at all completely new to law firms. Law firms and lawyers have been doing knowledge work, and knowledge management, since legal work first began. In every advice, in every transaction, in every call of a colleague to share an opinion or critique an idea, in every training session, in every practice team meeting, and in every work-related break-room conversation, lawyers have been building and sharing knowledge for centuries. Yet knowledge management has not always been a success in law firms, and knowledge management has become a challenge to firms that once had half a dozen employees but now have hundreds, or even thousands, of employees.

Law firms have always been pure knowledge businesses, always conscious of the fact that their sustainable advantage is the expertise and knowledge of their lawyers rather than any physical factors of production (Parsons, 2004). The growing awareness of knowledge and its value in organizations from the last decade of the twentieth century, coupled with the changes in the business environment, has resulted in progressive law firms investigating alternative ways of providing cost-efficient services that may sharpen their competitiveness and broaden their influence within the legal industry and the global economy. And so, more and more law firms and academic researchers have focused on KM in law firms.

Knowledge Organizations

A law firm is an organization specialized in the application of legal knowledge to client problems. The client may want to prevent a problem or solve a problem. In law firm work of prevention and solution, lawyers in the firm apply a variety of knowledge categories, such as declarative knowledge and procedural knowledge. Many law firms have transformed themselves from a professional model to a corporate business model. Knowledge is perceived as the resource upon which the business is based. Unique, inimitable, combinable, and exploitable knowledge provides competitive advantage. Thus, their primary resources stem from the human capital and social capital of the individuals employed within them.

A law firm is a business entity formed by one or more lawyers to engage in the practice of law. Law firms apply legal knowledge to clients' unique problems to provide a solution. At its core, the practice of law is the provision of specialized knowledge and services in a variety of ways. The primary service rendered by a law firm is advising clients (individuals, corporations, or authorities) about their legal rights and responsibilities and representing clients in civil or criminal cases, business transactions, and other matters in which legal advice and other assistance is sought.

In a resource perspective, where resources enable service innovation, knowledge and capabilities represent strategic resources that are integrated and configured by the service firm into its unique core competencies and organizational capabilities to achieve sustainable competitive advantage. Modes of innovation may vary, but knowledge-intensive business services require knowledge production directed at service innovation. Innovation in services very often includes creating applications of information technology.

Knowledge organizations have emerged as the dominant structure of both public and private organizations in the transition from an industrial to a knowledge society. Knowledge organization in the management sciences is concerned with structures within which knowledge workers solve knowledge problems.

Knowledge management research has described organizational knowledge flows in terms of the knowledge circulation process, consisting of five components: creation, accumulation, sharing, utilization, and internalization. Of these five parts, the knowledge sharing process is what this book focuses on. Knowledge sharing within and between organizations is not a one-way activity, but a process of trial and error, feedback, and mutual adjustment of both the source and the recipient of knowledge. This mutuality in knowledge sharing suggests that the process can be constructed as a sequence of collective actions in which the source and the recipient are involved. There are many different knowledge-sharing mechanisms: it can be informal and personal as well as formal and impersonal. Informal mechanisms include talk, unscheduled meetings, electronic bulletin boards, and discussion databases. More formal knowledge-sharing channels include video conferencing, training sessions, organizational intranets, and databases.

Knowledge organizations can be defined as complex adaptive systems composed of a large number of self-organizing components that seek to maximize their own goals but operate according to rules in the context of relationships with other components. In an intelligent complex adaptive system the agents are people. The systems (organizations) are frequently composed of hierarchical levels of self-organizing agents (or knowledge workers), which can take the forms of teams, divisions, or other structures that have common bonds. Thus while the components (knowledge workers) are self-organizing, they are not independent from the system they comprise (the professional organization).

Knowledge is often referred to as information combined with interpretation, reflection, and context. In cybernetics, knowledge is defined as a reducer of complexity or as a relation to predict and to select those actions that are necessary in establishing a competitive advantage for organizational survival. That is, knowledge is the capability to draw distinctions within a domain of actions. According to the knowledge-based view of the organization, the uniqueness of an organization's knowledge plays a fundamental role in its sustained ability to perform and succeed.

According to the knowledge-based theory of the firm, knowledge is the main resource for a firm's competitive advantage. Knowledge is the primary driver of a firm's value. Performance differences across firms can be attributed to the variance in the firms' strategic knowledge. Strategic knowledge is characterized by being valuable, unique, rare, inimitable, irreplaceable, nontransferable, combinable, and exploitable. Unlike other inert organizational resources, the application of existing knowledge has the potential to generate new knowledge.

Inherently, however, knowledge resides within individuals and, more specifically, in the employees who create, recognize, archive, access, and apply knowledge in carrying out their tasks. Consequently, the movement of knowledge across individual and organizational boundaries is dependent on employees' knowledge-sharing behaviors. However, extensive knowledge sharing within organizations still appears to be the exception rather than the rule.

The knowledge organization is very different from the bureaucratic organization. For example, the knowledge organization's focus on flexibility and customer response is very different from the bureaucracy's focus on organizational stability and the accuracy and repetitiveness of internal processes. In the knowledge organization, current practices emphasize using the ideas and capabilities of employees to improve decision making and organizational effectiveness. In contrast, bureaucracies utilize autocratic decision making by senior leadership with unquestioned execution by the workforce.

In knowledge organizations, transformational and charismatic leadership is an influential mode of leadership that is associated with high levels of individual and organizational performance. Leadership effectiveness is critically contingent on, and often defined in terms of, leaders' ability to motivate followers toward collective goals or a collective mission or vision.

In the knowledge society, knowledge organizations are expected to play a vital role in local economic development. For example, knowledge institutions such as universities are expected to stimulate regional and local economic development. Knowledge transfer units in universities such as Oxford in the UK and Grenoble in France are responsible for local and regional innovations.

The third characteristic of future knowledge organizations will be that of organizational intelligence. Organizational intelligence is the ability of an organization to perceive, interpret, and respond to its environment in a manner that meets its goals while satisfying multiple stakeholders. Intelligent behavior may be defined as being well prepared, providing excellent outcome-oriented thinking, choosing appropriate postures, and making outstanding decisions. Intelligent behavior includes acquiring knowledge continuously from all available resources and building it into an integrated picture, bringing together seemingly unrelated information to create new and unusual perspectives, and understanding the surrounding world.

In the context of law firms, intelligence has another meaning as well: it is information that is significant or potentially significant for an inquiry or potential inquiry. Intelligence is a subset of information, defined by the special quality of being significant and relevant. If information is significant, it has value and it has relevance. Analysis does not create intelligence; it merely discovers, attributes, and refines it.

Designing the knowledge organization of the future implies development of an intelligent complex adaptive system. In response to an environment of rapid change, increasing complexity, and great uncertainty, the organization of the future must become an adaptive organic business. The intelligent complex adaptive system will enter into a symbiotic relationship with its cooperative enterprise, virtual alliances, and external environment, while simultaneously retaining unity of purpose and effective identification and selection of incoming threats and opportunities.

In the knowledge organization, innovation and creativity are of critical importance. The literature on creativity provides a view of organizing for innovation by focusing on how individuals and teams come to shape knowledge in unique ways. Innovation consists of the creative generation of a new idea and the implementation of the idea into a valuable product, and thus creativity feeds innovation and is particularly critical in complex and interdependent work. Creativity can be viewed as the first stage of the overall innovation process.

Innovative solutions in the knowledge organization arise from diverse knowledge, processes that allow for creativity, and tasks directed toward creative solutions. Creativity requires application of deep knowledge because knowledge workers must understand the knowledge domain to push its boundaries. Team creativity likewise relies on tapping into the diverse knowledge of a team's members.

Within knowledge organizations, we often find communities of practice. For a variety of reasons, communities of practice seem a useful organizational subset for examining organizational knowledge as well as identity. First, such communities are privileged sites for a tight, effective loop of insight, problem identification, learning, and knowledge production. Second, they are significant repositories for the development, maintenance, and reproduction of knowledge. Third, community knowledge is more than the sum of its parts. Fourth, organizational ability to adapt to environmental change is often determined by communities of practice.

Knowledge resources, core competences, and dynamic capabilities are key drivers of service innovation in firms. Based on such drivers, a variety of modes of innovation emerge in knowledge-intensive business services. For example, distinctions can be made between the interactive innovation mode, the techno-organizational mode, the conservative mode, and the product innovation mode for knowledge-intensive business services:

- The interactive innovation mode occurs in the interaction with other firms and customers
- The techno-organizational mode occurs when technology adoption is not an isolated and passive strategy, but is closely intertwined with changes associated with the way in which services are provided and organized.
- The conservative mode occurs when a firm does not carry out any relevant innovation activity.
- The product innovation mode occurs when innovative ideas are linked to manufacturing.

The attention paid to the innovative activities of service sectors has probably increased over the last decade. Simultaneous production and consumption and the intangible nature of services make long-distance trade more difficult than for goods. This also gives a local flavor to competition, even when considering more sophisticated services. This is particularly evident in advanced regions, where competitiveness depends on knowledge content provided by highly specialized experts.

Therefore, knowledge production is increasingly directed at business services, emphasizing their role in innovative networks as carriers of knowledge and intermediaries between research (knowledge creator) and the customers (knowledge users). Knowledge-intensive business services are able to make existing knowledge useful for their customers, improving the customers' performance and productivity and contributing to technological and structural change.

In this context, knowledge-intensive business services are defined in terms of service characteristics and knowledge characteristics. Among service characteristics, we find close interaction between service provider and customer, as there is a highly intangible content of service products and processes. Among knowledge characteristics, we find the ability to receive information from outside the firm and to transform this information together with firm-specific knowledge into useful services for customers.

Sometimes there is a service-dominant logic in resource management. Researchers apply resource-advantage theory to suggest marketing's evolution toward a new dominant logic that requires the focus of marketing to be on the intangible, dynamic, operant resources that are the heart of competitive advantage and performance.

Drawing from the resources, competences, resource-advantage theory, capabilities, and dynamic capabilities literature, researchers have extended and elaborated on the service-dominant logic's notion of operant resources by proposing a hierarchy of operant resources. Starting from the seven basic resource categories (financial, physical, legal, human, organizational, informational, and relational), they propose basic, composite, and interconnected operant resources as the hierarchy.

Innovation in services very often includes creative application of information technology found in the technological dimension of innovation. However, innovation in services is becoming an increasingly complex issue in which the adoption of information and communication technology is just one of many possible facilitators.

A number of important concepts have been introduced in this chapter, including knowledge, knowledge management, core competencies, and dynamic capabilities. These concepts represent perspectives to gain insights into barriers and enablers of service innovation. At the center of these concepts we find knowledge as a resource to be explored and exploited for the benefit of innovation in services.

Learning Organizations

While knowledge workers develop knowledge, organizations learn. Therefore, "learning organization" has become a frequently used term. The learning organization is similar to knowledge development. While knowledge development is taking place at the individual level, organizational learning is taking place at the firm level. Organizational learning occurs when the firm is able to exploit individual competence in new and innovative ways. Organizational learning also occurs when the collective memory—including local language, common history, and routines—expands. Organizational learning causes growth in the intellectual capital. Learning is a continuous process of knowledge creation. A learning organization is a place where people are constantly driven to discover what has caused the current situation and how they can change it. To maintain competitive advantage, an organization's investment decisions related to knowledge creation are likely to be strategic in nature.

Some scholars argue that the real knowledge organization is the learning organization. A learning organization is one that changes as a result of its experiences. Under the best of circumstances, these changes result in performance improvements. The terms *knowledge organization* and *learning organization* are usually (but not necessarily) used to describe service organizations. This is because most, if not all, of the value of these organizations comes from how well their professionals learn from the environment, diagnose problems, and then work with clients or customers to improve their situations. The problems with which they work are frequently ambiguous and unstructured. The information, skills, and experience needed to address these problems vary with work cases. Thus, the need for learning and obtaining new knowledge is recognized. A typical example is the work of lawyers in law firms.

Similarly, some scholars argue that learning and knowledge will become two of the three most important emergent characteristics of future world-class organization. Learning will be continuous and widespread, utilizing mentoring, classroom, and distance learning and will likely be self-managed with strong infrastructure support. The creation, storage, transfer, and application of knowledge will have been refined and developed such that it becomes a major resource of the organization as it satisfies customers and adapts to environmental competitive forces and opportunities.

The learning organization is a concept of the ideal organization with its own capacity to learn and, therefore, the ability to change. The concept relies on the assumption that learning is a means to reach a goal, not the goal itself. That is why learning organizations focus on change leading to learning. More recent approaches within the area of organizational learning are more concerned with learning as an ongoing process of change, where learning is both the goal and the means.

Continuous improvements are to be achieved based on experience. Change in resources, activities, and approaches occur in the organization on a continuous basis. Communication channels are expanded internally (*intra*-organization) as well as externally (*inter*-organization). An organizational culture of sharing, transparency, and contribution is stimulated. At this stage, demand-side knowledge management replaces supply-side knowledge management. Here knowledge sources are familiar to everyone, and knowledge sharing occurs on demand for that knowledge. This represents an important step in effectiveness improvement, as knowledge is only shared when knowledge is needed.

Sharing knowledge is an important element in making a law firm a learning organization. Clients of a law firm have come to expect exceptional service, including rapid and robust communication, knowledge sharing, and efficient and effective collaboration among the best and the brightest in the firm.

Value Shop Configuration

The value shop creation logic is problem solving by the change from an existing to a more desired state. There are five generic categories of primary value shop activities, illustrated in Figure 5.1.

- Problem finding and acquisition. Activities associated with the recording, reviewing and formulating of the problem to be solved and choosing the overall approach to solving the problem;
- Problem-solving. Activities associated with generating and evaluating alternative solutions;
- Choice. Activities associated with choosing among alternative problem solutions;
- Execution. Activities associated with communicating, organizing, and implementing the chosen solution;
- Control and evaluation. Activities associated with measuring and evaluating to what extent implementation has solved the initial statement.

Value creation logic determines priorities and resource allocation. The value that might be created by working on and solving a

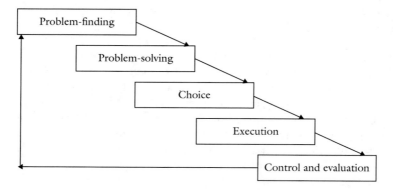

Figure 5.1 Value configuration activities in a law firm as value shop

problem determines how each problem is perceived and understood. A value organization makes strategic decisions about the role of the organization as it relates to the specter of problems with which it is confronted. Performance goals are important at this stage, where goal setting is part of the strategy process, while goal achievement is part of the management process.

Entrepreneurship for Organizational Capabilities

Corporate entrepreneurship is crucial in the acquisition of dynamic organizational capabilities. Scholars have identified entrepreneurship as the core process by which companies have attempted to redefine, renew, and remake themselves.

An entrepreneurship perspective on the nature of the firm rests on two fundamental assumptions about the nature of business activity: profit-seeking individuals and asymmetrically dispersed knowledge across economic actors. The quest for profit, wealth, and power plays an important motivational role in the entrepreneur's pursuit of new business opportunities. Asymmetrically dispersed knowledge implies differentiated sets of knowledge held by decision makers, which in the business context causes variation in the ability to identify and assimilate new information and events. Individual decision makers tend to notice new information that relates to and can be combined with knowledge they already have.

An entrepreneur is a person who operates a new enterprise or venture or revitalizes an existing enterprise and assumes some accountability for the inherent risk. Entrepreneurship is often difficult and tricky, as many new ventures fail. In the context of the creation of for-profit enterprises, "entrepreneur" is often synonymous with founder. Most commonly, the term *entrepreneur* applies to someone who creates value by offering a product or service in order to obtain certain profit. Entrepreneurship is thus the practice of starting new organizations or revitalizing mature organizations, particularly new businesses, generally in response to identified opportunities. Entrepreneurship is sometimes labeled entrepreneurialism. Entrepreneurial activity is substantially different from operational activity as it is mainly concerned with creativity and innovation. Entrepreneurship ranges from small individual initiatives to major undertakings creating many job opportunities.

The majority of recent theories in the business and managerial economic literature assume that the economic performance of small and medium-sized firms depends largely on the entrepreneurs' (or team's) capacities. Even so, economists still do not fully understand the relationship between entrepreneurs and firm performance. The entrepreneurial process is the result of a complex interaction between individual, social, and environmental factors. Taken separately, neither the personality of the entrepreneur nor the structural characteristics of the environment can, on its own, determine an organization's performance.

In order to provide an example of the relationship between entrepreneurs' subjective characteristics/traits and organizational performance, researchers carried out an empirical study. The study aimed to explain how the presence of entrepreneurs' specific subjective characteristics can influence an organization's strategic orientation and, as a consequence, local development. By analyzing several subjective characteristics taken from a sample of 101 successful entrepreneurs from southern Italy, certain issues emerged regarding the link between the economic performance of the ventures launched in this area and the weak level of growth. Successful entrepreneurs' behavior and decisions seemed heavily influenced by family support. The entrepreneurial culture of the family also tends to substitute the protective role played by public institutions. The entrepreneurial decisions of local entrepreneurs are triggered both by their need to rid themselves of poverty and their feeling that they are destined to continue the family business, the majority of them being the children of entrepreneurs. Most of the interviewees were classified as necessity rather than opportunity entrepreneurs.

Entrepreneurs might be driven by a compulsive need to find new ways of allocating resources. They might be searching for profit-making opportunities and engineer incremental changes in products and processes. While strongly innovative entrepreneurs tend to champion radical changes in resource allocation by making new service markets and pioneering new processes, weakly innovative entrepreneurs tend to seek small changes in resource allocation to explore profit-making opportunities between already established activities.

Founders of new legal firms tend to be experienced professionals who pursue opportunities closely related to their previous employment. Entrepreneurs often have several years of work experience in the same industry as their own start-up enterprises. This suggests that entrepreneurs do not come from out of the blue, but build their human intellectual capital through work experience in established firms. Similarly, criminal entrepreneurs might be experienced professionals before establishing their own criminal business enterprise.

How do entrepreneurs choose their boundaries of their own ventures? To answer this question, researchers started from the premise that, while entrepreneurs believe themselves to have superior ideas in one or multiple parts of value creation arenas, they are characteristically short of cash and of the ability to convince others to provide it. This premise motivates a simple model in which the entrepreneur has a value-adding set of ideas for parts of a value-creation arena. Assuming that the entrepreneur's objective is to maximize wealth, it might be observed that initial scope depends on available cash, but also on how much value the entrepreneur's ideas add to each participant in the enterprise. Entrepreneurs will focus on the areas that provide the maximum profit and minimum risk per available cash in service innovation.

6

Knowledge Management in Law Firms

Law firms exist because they can coordinate collective learning more efficiently and effectively than individual lawyers can. In particular, if organization-specific knowledge is required to perform a task, using the external market becomes increasingly inefficient since an external supplier would first have to adopt this knowledge before being able to perform that task (Dibbern et al., 2008). This is in line with the knowledge-based view of the firm, which is the theoretical perspective applied in this book.

The knowledge-based view assumes that knowledge integration processes occur within the law firm. Knowledge integration processes involve social interaction among individuals using internal communication channels for knowledge transfer and knowledge development to arrive at a common perspective for problem solving. Where organizational units hold specialized knowledge, inter-unit linkages are the primary means of transferring that knowledge. Such knowledge transfer permits knowledge reuse, and the recombination of existing knowledge is an important antecedent of uncertainty resolution in organizational service innovation.

Definitions of Knowledge Management

There is no single definition of knowledge management, but in general the idea relates to unlocking and leveraging the knowledge of individuals so that this knowledge becomes available as an organizational resource that is not dependent on the particular individual to be applied in an organization's business. Much of the literature on knowledge management is driven from an information systems perspective and is based on the belief that KM systems can be used to capture and stockpile workers' knowledge and make it accessible to others via a searchable application. However, as argued in this book, knowledge and wisdom can only be stored in the human brain, while data and information can be stored in computers.

Similar to knowledge, there is still no universally accepted definition of knowledge management. Several factors appear to have influenced the diverse definitions of knowledge management. First, there is a wide difference in perspectives of the subject from different authors. For example, some may have a human resources perspective, while others may have a systems perspective. Second, knowledge management is looked at from a wide spectrum of disciplines, such as economics, sociology, philosophy, psychology, management, information technology, and information science each attributing different meanings to the term. Third, it is also a collection of concepts borrowed from information management, artificial intelligence, knowledge support systems, software engineering, business process re-engineering, personnel training, learning, and organizational behavior. Fourth, the phrase "knowledge management" implies that knowledge can be managed, when in reality the management of knowledge is about the management of people, processes, and systems through which knowledge can be shared. Finally, like knowledge, knowledge management is an evolving, broad, vague, conceptual, recursive, and highly theoretical concept.

Because there are so many definitions of knowledge management, the following definitions are just a representative sample of what has been suggested in knowledge management literature. For example, KM mainly involves the processes of identifying what information and knowledge a lawyer needs and where it can be found, then making that information and knowledge available in the required format in a suitable fashion. Furthermore, knowledge management is to organize and manage operational processes within the knowledge value chain in such a way that realization of the organization's collective ambition, objectives, and strategy is advanced. Also, KM is a framework and tool set for improving the organization's knowledge infrastructure, aimed at getting the right knowledge to the right people in the right form at the right time.

Furthermore, knowledge management is the leveraging of a firm's collective wisdom by creating systems and processes to support and facilitate the identification, capture, dissemination, and use of the firm's knowledge to meet business objectives. Knowledge management can be understood as the name given to a set of systematic and disciplined actions that an organization can take to obtain the greatest value from the knowledge available to it. KM is not only based on the management of information and knowledge, but also entails managing the balance of people, processes, and technology that determines the organization and its relationship with its markets and other stakeholders. It is about creating an environment where knowledge, creativity, and innovation are valued by facilitating communication between people in different locations and from different departments and creating an organization that encourages ideas and rewards success while also allowing people to fail and learn from failure. KM might also include all efforts to optimize the achievements of organizations by controlling knowledge. Knowledge management is a young discipline that helps to reduce costs and mistakes of organizations, to increase the commitment of employees, and to improve the communication between employees.

There are a number of approaches to knowledge management in the literature. Wang (2009) describes these approaches as schools of knowledge management strategy:

- *Systems school*: The systems school strategies aim to capture and store information based on knowledge of individuals in knowledge support repositories. This implies that the fundamental concerns of the system school are the creation and codification of knowledge.
- *Cartographic school*: The cartographic school strategies focus on mapping knowledge by creating directories of knowledge owners, like a yellow pages. When people need certain kinds of knowledge, they look in the yellow pages to find who has the knowledge needed and how this person can be reached.
- *Process school*: The process school strategies aim to provide people not only with the knowledge they request but also with the most useful knowledge that is relevant to their current tasks. This implies an approach to equip individuals with the knowledge they need to effectively perform their tasks.
- *Commercial school*: The commercial school strategies support the concept of managing knowledge as an asset and stress the importance of organizations' capabilities with recognizing the economic value of their knowledge.
- *Organizational school*: The organizational school strategies aim to facilitate knowledge management activities by designing

organizational structures or inter-organizational networks that connect knowledge owners for sharing knowledge.
- *Spatial school*: Spatial school strategies take advantage of the use of space to facilitate knowledge exchange. Socialization, such as face-to-face contact, is critical since it accounts for a significant proportion of the transferred knowledge.
- *Strategic school*: The strategic school strategies aim to examine the knowledge preserved by an organization in order to determine what competitive advantages the organization can generate by utilizing its knowledge. This knowledge is valued as a key organizational resource.

Knowledge management and intellectual capital are different but related issues that are most often used interchangeably. While intellectual capital is concerned with measuring the value of knowledge in the organization, knowledge management is concerned with developing this value. Like knowledge management, the practical management objective of intellectual capital is to convert human capital (individual and group learning) to structural capital (organizational knowledge or what is left when people go home, such as documented processes and a knowledge base), thereby reducing the risk of losing valuable knowledge when people leave the organization. A disadvantage of capital approaches is that they ignore the political and social aspects of knowledge management, such as reward and recognition, power, relations, and empowerment resulting in a simplistic mechanized approach to complex social issues.

Knowledge management can be looked at from many different points of view. Points of view are, for example, KM for organizations and KM support for the execution of legal tasks. The most popular, and usually the only, point of view for KM is its deployment to support an entire organization. In this view, KM is mainly approached top-down. This approach is, in our view and at least in the legal domain, presently too complex and too limited. The complexity becomes clear when we look at current literature on KM in which vague and global notions of KM are used to describe knowledge management. To be able to apply KM to an entire organization, we need to reduce the complexity of the organization as a whole and look at smaller parts of the organization and its tasks. With smaller parts we mean divisions of organizations and employees performing legal tasks. Furthermore, we need to focus on each individual knowledge worker as a human being with desires, feelings, ambitions, and motives. We call this approach a bottom-up approach. With the help of KM for small parts of the organization, it should become easier to develop a knowledge management method for the entire organization and apply it. With regard to a top-down approach being too limited, KM in law firms should be multidimensional—top-down, bottom-up, and inside-out.

Knowledge management is a way to contribute to the business objective of many law firms: increase profitability by working more effectively, leverage expertise, improve productivity, stop reinventing the wheel, come up with innovative solutions, enjoy problem solving, and make available the necessary resources to support the needs of the firm.

My research shows that the concept of KM is well understood in a Norwegian law firm, Thommessen, as responding lawyers were asked to express their own definitions of knowledge management:

- Combine experience and data/information in an effective business process
- Make information more available to all
- Systematic collection and storage of knowledge for reuse by others
- Make knowledge accessible
- Organize the knowledge we already have
- Collect and present information from various sources
- Managing and structuring information/data so that data/info become available
- How to manage our knowledge resource
- Development of new competencies
- Shared memory of the organization
- Utilization of the tools we have.

Interviews with lawyers from Dutch law firms also indicate that, while there is no universally accepted definition of knowledge management in law firms, there is indeed an understanding of what it is all about.

Benefits of Knowledge Management

Significantly more law firms and academic researchers have focused on knowledge management in law firms. Benefits of KM for law firms include:

- KM will allow a firm to produce certain documents more efficiently, thus resulting in a higher level of service.

- If specialist knowledge is captured in a document or system as information, it allows a firm to provide more complete and higher quality service to their clients.
- Efficient and effective KM makes life much easier for lawyers and can result in increased productivity and reduced stress.
- Capturing knowledge in the form of information and data in a computer system allows it to remain if an individual leaves the firm.
- Tailor-made KM aids in the transfer of knowledge between lawyers by electronically handling the documents for them, thus ensuring knowledge is retained and made available for reuse.
- Effective KM can assist in the integration of new lawyers into the firm, such as graduates from law school learning the trade by studying cases electronically stored in databases and collections of databases in a data warehouse.
- KM is a necessary component of risk management. Effective transfer of knowledge may help avoid professional negligence suits.
- KM helps stimulate creativity and knowledge development and creation, since access to a variety of information sources both internally and externally is provided to lawyers.

For these reasons, if a firm wants to survive and prosper in a competitive market, it is essential that it not only implements a KM program, but also continuously improves knowledge sharing and knowledge creation. Successful KM allows lawyers to be more effective and productive knowledge workers who provide better service to their clients.

Successful KM in law firms can thus lead to quicker problem solving, better decision making, and enhanced customer relations— especially if customers are directly or indirectly linked to law firm information sources— thereby providing improved client service. Productivity and efficiency can improve, thereby enabling a higher hourly rate for the firm and/or lower costs for the client. Knowledge sharing helps colleagues learn from each other, thereby avoiding mistakes and work redundancies. Researching new legal topics might be supported by knowledge management functions.

While knowledge management improves exchanges between lawyers and thus interdependencies between colleagues, at the same time it increases lawyer work independence. Work independence is of concern both in time and space: a lawyer might like to work on a case at a different point in time and at a different location than a coworker who is on the same case.

The external effects of successful KM in a law firm also include market visibility among potential clients as well as attractiveness for the best students graduating from law schools. If clients are enabled to link their own work processes into law firm work processes, then a synergy is established, such that one might expect loyalty from clients—especially larger accounts and corporate clients—over time.

If the KM system includes competence profiles and workload scheduling, then it provides the ability to direct work to skilled specialists who are currently available. This allows fee earners to create a more stable workload for themselves. Reduced frustration and time in searching documents can be expected. This, in turn, might lead to job satisfaction, more collaborative training, simplified processes, forward planning and again—as a result—improved client service.

Since knowledge management is not a fad but a trend that has caused turbulence and paradigm shifts in the legal industry all over the world, it is important for each law firm to benefit from, rather than be surprised by, this way of working. In the past, lawyers were confident that they knew the sources of knowledge in the legal profession. Those sources were stable and did not change. Lawyers knew where to find the casebooks, law books, and client files. Books were on the shelf behind the desk, while files were in the filing cabinet next to the desk or in the secretariat. Law work was extremely individual. Because of pressure to know more, knowledge cooperation rather than competition has to become the rule and not the exception in all law firms.

Now it is all on the screen in front of the lawyer, on the desk. The lawyer does not control the sources, although it is indeed possible to store and file locally what might be needed to do today's and tomorrow's knowledge work. In the past, the lawyer or the secretary knew where to find forms that had been created for use in stockholder arrangements, tax calculations, transactions, and other document-based work. Today, firms have access to a variety of forms from a variety of sources as they grow locally as well as globally.

In the past, it was possible in most firms for lawyers to pop their heads around colleagues' doors and ask, "Has anyone done one of these or seen one of these before?" Although some firms do simulate this process using e-mail, it has often caused more harm than help. This is because firms have grown larger: There may be hundreds of lawyers and other staff in the firm, and they all read e-mail, even when the request is only relevant to one or two people, stealing time from the others.

Hundreds of lawyers and other staff require an organizational structure that often lead to clusters of rather self-contained islands, with insufficient sharing of know-what, know-how, and know-why. Successful knowledge management has the ability to compensate and bridge islands by free access to all information sources independent of origin in different departments and functions.

As legal information and guidance become available on the global information infrastructure, many individuals and organizations beyond the legal profession are likely to want to compete in this profitable marketplace and provide legal and quasi-legal services themselves. Accountancy firms, auditing firms, consulting firms, and electronic publishers are progressing. However, when a client has a problem of substantial value, then the choice of service provider will be determined by quality and reputation only held by leading law firms. Thus, benefits from knowledge management to established law firms will be found in competing successfully with external competitors, such as auditing and consulting firms on information processing, while at the same time being the winner in quality of legal advice.

Processes in Knowledge Management

Distinctions can be made between obtaining knowledge, creating knowledge, and sharing knowledge. The process of obtaining knowledge is important for law firms. Should a lawyer become unable to perform his or her duties, or should the lawyer's office become destroyed, sufficient information and knowledge must exist in other locations to enable work continuation and completion. The individualization of knowledge work that makes continuation and completion of a given task completely dependent on one single individual in the firm is not always acceptable to the client. More common are situations in which lawyers need to obtain bits of knowledge from various sources in a reasonable amount of time to put together a proposal or some other form of legal advice.

The second process, knowledge creation, involves developing new content or replacing existing content within the organization's tacit and explicit knowledge. Through social and collaborative processes as well as individuals' cognitive processes, knowledge is created. Knowledge creation is often a spiral of activities that switch between explicit knowledge shared by others and implicit knowledge carried with each individual. Over time, this spiral causes new knowledge to emerge, as individuals share their thinking, their reasoning, their reflections, and their conclusions. It is often a growing spiral flow as knowledge moves through individual, group, and organizational levels.

Four elements of knowledge creation have been identified. First, socialization occurs: each individual understands what is being communicated by others. Next, internalization occurs, as each individual thinks about what has been said or read. Then, with externalization, each individual communicates new thoughts about the subject. Finally combination occurs, when communicated knowledge from several individuals is combined in the form of explicit knowledge. This spiral was first suggested by Japanese researchers and later translated into different knowledge organization settings. For example, this research in Japan suggests that the essential question of knowledge creation is establishing an organization's *ba*, defined as a common place or space for creating knowledge. Four types of *ba* corresponding to the four modes of knowledge creation are identified: origination, interacting, cyber, and exercising. Originating *ba* entails the socialization mode of knowledge creation and is the *ba* from which the organizational knowledge creation process begins.

The third process, knowledge sharing within and between organizations, is not a one-way activity, but a process of trial and error, feedback, and mutual adjustment of both the source and the recipient of knowledge. This mutuality in knowledge sharing suggests that the process can be constructed as a sequence of collective actions in which the source and the recipient are involved.

There are many different knowledge-sharing mechanisms: it can be informal and personal as well as formal and impersonal. Informal mechanisms include talk, unscheduled meetings, electronic bulletin boards, and discussion databases. More formal knowledge sharing channels include video conferencing, training sessions, organizational intranets, and databases.

Knowledge sharing is a knowledge process to support employees in executing tasks such as solving a problem. During this process various tools play a role, such as language, gestures, illustrations, and information technology. The process encompasses stimulating the sharing of experience, ideas, and thoughts between people. It is the process in which individuals collectively share their knowledge and collectively may develop new knowledge as well. Sharing knowledge implies that every knowledge-sharing process consists of bringing or donating knowledge as well as collecting knowledge.

Sharing knowledge takes place at different levels within an organization: between individuals, by individuals with explicit sources, between individuals and groups, between groups, among group members, and from a group to the organization. Knowledge sharing and collaboration are closely related. Knowledge that cannot be communicated and shared with others is nearly useless. Knowledge becomes useful and actionable when shared throughout an organization and between collaborating organizations. Successful knowledge sharing not only concerns knowledge sharing within one's own section, but also outside sections and even outside the firm. Legal domains often overlap. A lawyer in a large law firm can receive an assignment that covers multiple legal domains. This lawyer may know all about one legal domain but may have less experience with a legal subfield. To deliver high-quality advice, sufficient knowledge of all legal domains involved is necessary. Because legal domains can be handled by various sections within a law firm, knowledge sharing between sections is important.

For the same reason as knowledge sharing *within* the section, a lawyer takes care that, when learning something new, colleagues outside the section can learn the same. Lawyers also share their knowledge with colleagues outside their own sections. On the other hand colleagues from other sections also share what they know.

Knowledge Sharing in Law Firms

Lawyers in a law firm consult each other, challenge each other, and make friends with each other. They meet during lunch, in front of the coffee machine, in the hallway, or during a formal meeting. This behavior supports the personalization strategy of knowledge management. The codification strategy of knowledge management finds support when lawyers search internal databases, websites, and communicate online. Because of an increased availability and use of IT, it has become so much easier to publish massive amounts of information and knowledge. This creates both an opportunity and a problem. The opportunity is that relevant information is most likely out there; however, finding it is another story. Effective and efficient knowledge sharing could help to relieve this information overload.

Furthermore, law firms have grown, sometimes due to mergers or expansion into (inter)national markets. Because of this growth, the structure and overview of the firm becomes more complex, so it becomes harder for lawyers to find relevant experts or expertise. Clients also want better quality and service in shorter time, so sharing knowledge within the firm becomes essential. Last but not least, we see that new legal problems emerge, as well as new laws and regulations, for many reasons, including, for example, as a consequence of new development on the Internet. Having the right knowledge at the right time to deal with new developments is another example of why it is not a surprise that researchers and law firms have become more interested in knowledge management generally and knowledge sharing in particular.

Law firms and lawyers cannot afford spending time re-inventing the wheel every time clients have similar problems. Because several individuals in different departments within an organization possess knowledge, sharing it is a requirement for the combination and development of knowledge. Sharing knowledge between lawyers improves the economic benefits a law firm can realize from the knowledge of their lawyers. Sharing of knowledge is becoming increasingly important because a network of lawyers can significantly come up with better legal advice than any individual lawyer. Cooperation without hiding important knowledge will result in more productivity and innovation than anyone could reach individually.

Resource-Based Theory of Knowledge Management

The above arguments for knowledge sharing in law firms are very much in line with the resource-based theory of the firm, where knowledge is identified as the most important resource. According to the resource-based theory of the firm, performance differences across firms can be attributed to the variance in the firms' resources and capabilities. Knowledge that is valuable, unique, difficult to imitate, combinable, difficult to substitute, and exploitable can provide the basis for firms' competitive advantages. The essence of the resource-based theory of the firm lies in its emphasis on the internal resources—here, knowledge—available to the firm, rather than on the external opportunities and threats dictated by industry conditions and market change.

The essence of the resource-based theory of the enterprise lies in its emphasis on the internal resources available to the enterprise, rather than on the external opportunities and threats dictated by industry conditions. Enterprises are considered to be highly heterogeneous, and the bundles of resources available to each enterprise are different. This is both because enterprises have different initial resource endowments and because managerial decisions affect resource accumulation and the direction of enterprise growth as well as resource utilization. The resource-based view of the firm posits that firm competitiveness comes from unique bundles of tangible and intangible assets that are valuable, rare, imperfectly imitable, irreplaceable, combinable, and sustainable.

Knowledge is the major resource in most companies. From a resource perspective, knowledge sharing is important in law firms for several reasons. First, knowledge sharing helps prevent colleagues needlessly applying outdated or irrelevant knowledge, leading to incorrect or substandard advice. Whether a client has a "good case" or a "bad case" is an initial assessment very much based on updated and complete knowledge. Next, wasting time is avoided if it turns out that someone else has solved the same problem in the past. Furthermore, the chance of conflicting interests decreases. Also, knowledge sharing leads to educational savings.

However, empirical research does show that knowledge sharing in law firms leaves plenty of room for improvement. In most law firms there is a limited focus on capturing and sharing tacit knowledge. Lawyers are not really encouraged to share what they have learned from their recent assignments with others, and senior staff is too busy to reflect on their experiences and share them. Few firms have a well-organized system for sharing knowledge within and across departments or practice areas, and sharing knowledge systematically is hardly part of the culture in law firms. The lack of time seems to be the most important obstacle among lawyers in a culture that does not support knowledge sharing. However, the lack of time is also an excuse often accepted, although it is not always relevant. Sometimes, the busiest and most profitable lawyers are also the greatest contributors to knowledge sharing, while less busy and less profitable lawyers are not. One reason for this behavior can be found in the lower self-confidence in the second group.

Lawyers tend to agree that they share knowledge within their own departments, but they do not share much knowledge outside them. Talking informally to colleagues and asking for advice helps to establish relationships among people, especially when it comes to collaboration across business units and national borders.

Transaction Cost Theory of Knowledge Sharing

While we have stressed the importance of knowledge sharing in large and growing law firms, there are limits to the extent knowledge sharing is beneficial to the firm. To understand knowledge sharing limitations, we apply transaction cost theory. Transaction cost theory argues that if the costs of obtaining knowledge from others is too high, then it is more relevant to apply the knowledge one already has. Costs are measured in terms of time, effort, problems, communication, and other elements that make knowledge transfer difficult or even impossible.

There are several reasons why knowledge sharing is associated with high transaction costs in law firms. First, individuality in law firms implies that each professional is independent of colleagues in her work. By nature, law firms tend to foster a culture of individual practices. This individuality of lawyers complicates knowledge sharing. Lawyers and their departments within the firm generally consider themselves—or want to consider themselves—as self-employed. In fact, departments sometimes compete with each other.

Lawyers are not typically recognized for a team-based approach to legal work; they are not noted for their team-oriented attitude toward legal work or for their willingness to share their expertise. This individuality is encouraged as partner compensation models reward the individual, not the firm. Thus, there is often limited interaction between practice groups in law firms. Individuality is also characterized by a knowledge-is-power culture in law firms. Lawyers tend to think that their work is unique and is of little or no value to others. Individuality may also be encouraged by a decentralized culture and a limited training and mentoring of junior lawyers in law firms.

Individuality of lawyers occurs because lawyers, as knowledge workers, can only be managed to the extent they consent to be managed. Individuality expresses itself in law firms because lawyers, as professionals, have specialized knowledge and have been trained as elites. Some practice groups within law firms may have such specialized practices that their knowledge would be of interest primarily or even exclusively only to them. This is an example of the individuality of lawyers as it creates an information- silos problem only to the extent there is a problem when information is not being shared throughout the firm.

Another reason why knowledge sharing is associated with high transaction costs is the structure of incentives and rewards practiced by most law firms. The way employees in a firm are rewarded strongly influences the attitude with regard to the sharing of knowledge. In most law firms, few financial incentives for lawyers exist to share knowledge with colleagues. On the contrary, extensive time spent on knowledge sharing may lead to reduced individual income, thus representing transaction costs.

A third kind of transaction cost occurs when the relative power of a lawyer diminishes as that lawyer lets others learn the same kind of skills and gain the same kind of insights. Among professionals, knowledge is part of their skillset, and skills offer the lawyer power. A lot of power remains at the bottom of the hierarchy, with the lawyers themselves. As a result, sharing too much knowledge could mean that lawyers might have to share their power. And often that power in the form of knowledge is needed to progress in the firm—for example to become partner. Some lawyers do indeed see their knowledge as part of their power. By not sharing their knowledge, they feel they can keep this power. Therefore we find a knowledge-is-power culture in some law firms. Many lawyers feel that their careers depend on their ability to develop a unique set of knowledge and, therefore, might hoard their knowledge. Knowledge can be used to take action and to enforce spheres of influence. To pass knowledge to colleagues might grant some of these abilities. Those who do not have this knowledge are deprived of the capacity to act or to influence.

Some practice groups may have such specialized practices that their knowledge may be of interest primarily to them. In some law firms, lawyers are competing directly with each other through their specialized knowledge, gifts, and talents. As a consequence, lawyers may be very cautious about openly sharing their knowledge with colleagues for fear that they possibly give up an individual leading edge. Often competition and incentives for individual performance urge lawyers to build unique expertise in a certain area and to isolate that expertise for their own, personal clients. Sometimes lawyers have high levels of political activity within the firm. Power expresses itself in the form of partners who are the owners of the business and have passed a number of hurdles to partnership that confirm them as being special. They like to be treated differently to acknowledge their position and status. Here we find the mentality of some lawyers who might hoard their knowledge in light of the belief that knowledge is power.

Individuality, incentives, and power are reasons why knowledge sharing is associated with high transaction costs in law firms. A fourth reason is the extent of uncertainty. Many lawyers worry about criticism of their knowledge by colleagues and careless use of their knowledge by colleagues in the firm. Thus, transaction costs emerge in the form of criticism and careless use. Especially younger and less experienced colleagues may feel uncertain because they cannot judge if their working results and experiences represent valuable knowledge for others, and they do not know what will be said about their work among influential partners. They cannot estimate if their knowledge is too general or too well known or—on the other side—that some results are too specific for a special situation and therefore useless for colleagues in other situations. Some lawyers feel that they have to deliver custom-made advice and so do not want to make use of the colleagues' knowledge, where transaction costs arise as wasting time. For some lawyers it is also difficult to understand colleagues' knowledge, meaning that transaction costs arise as wasting time in trying to understand what others have done.

Fifth, a lack of motivation can be found in many law firms, where lawyers are not really motivated by management ideals to share their knowledge. Rather, they think they represent a business in the business where they can do as they like, as long as they make money. Sharing knowledge in law firms is often seen as additional work because of the time necessary for reflection, documentation, communication, and socialization. Some lawyers do not expect reciprocal benefits from sharing because they do not believe in these benefits or they did not experience it so far. And even if lawyers do expect payback for their contributions, the somehow natural human question—what's in it for me—is often not clear to knowledge workers, who then suffer from a lack of motivation.

Sixth, the most limited resource for many lawyers, is time. And time is usually money. Sharing complex and specialist knowledge asks for time in which there is room for personal interaction and documentation of the knowledge. Being at the same place at the same time to clarify contents of knowledge may represent too high transaction costs. Thus, lawyers feel too busy for prioritizing knowledge sharing. Lawyers prioritize their nonbillable time quite carefully. Time spent sharing knowledge and experience is normally time not spent billing clients. In fact, lawyers may be penalized for their efforts at knowledge transfer, if it has the effect of reducing their billable hours, again representing unacceptable transaction costs to many knowledge workers. Overcoming time constraints, especially the emphasis on billable hours, is generally a barrier for new initiatives in law firms. The time-based billing model seems to be the greatest cultural barrier to developing and implementing more extensive knowledge management.

There are many more reasons why knowledge sharing is associated with high transaction costs in law firms. As a result of the individualistic nature of law firms, there is a lack of sufficient trust and loyalty between colleagues and the firm to accommodate effective knowledge transfer. Often, knowledge workers need to know each other to trust each other. However, in a large law firm of hundreds of lawyers, personal relationships are not possible with all colleagues Therefore, fear of peer judgment among lawyers emerges from the unknown. Thus, building trust and protecting knowledge are two bottlenecks in law firms, representing two sides of the same coin. Without a high level of mutual trust, employees will be skeptical about the intentions and behaviors of others, and they will probably hold on to their knowledge.

7

Theoretical Perspectives on Defense Lawyers

It is difficult to overstate the importance of theory to understand white-collar crime lawyers and attorney-client relationships. Theory allows analysts to understand and predict outcomes on the basis of probability. Theory also allows analysts to describe and explain a process or sequence of events. Theory prevents analysts from being bewildered by the complexity of the real world by providing a linguistic tool for organizing a coherent understanding of the real world.

Accordingly, theory acts as an educational device that creates insights into criminal phenomena (Colquitt and Zapata-Phelan, 2007):

> A theory might be a prediction or explanation, a set of interrelated constructs, definitions, and propositions that presents a systematic view of phenomena by specifying relations among variables, with the purpose of explaining natural phenomena. The systematic view might be an argument, a discussion, or a rationale, and it helps to explain or predict phenomena that occur in the world. Some define theory in terms of relationships between independent and dependent variables, where theory is a collection of assertions, both verbal and symbolic, that identifies what variables are important and for what reasons, and that specifies how they are interrelated and why. It identifies the conditions under which variables should be related or not related. Other scholars have defined theory in terms of narratives and accounts.

Sutton and Staw (1995) define theory in the following way:

> Theory is about the connections among phenomena, a story about why acts, events, structure, and thoughts occur. Theory emphasizes the nature of causal relationships, identifying what comes first as well as the timing of such events. Strong theory, in our view, probes underlying processes

so as to understand the systematic reasons for a particular occurrence or nonoccurrence. It often burrows deeply into micro processes, laterally into neighboring concepts, or in an upward direction, tying itself to broader social phenomena. It usually is laced with a set of convincing and logically interconnected arguments. It can have implications that we have not seen with our naked (or theoretically unassisted) eye. It may have implications that run counter to our common sense (378).

A theory is often a statement predicting which actions will lead to what results and why. Every action that defense lawyers take, and every plan they formulate, is based on some theory in the backs of their minds that makes them expect the actions they contemplate will lead to the results they envision (Christensen and Raynor, 2003).

According to Christensen and Raynor, the construction of a solid theory proceeds in three stages. It begins with a description of some phenomenon we wish to understand, in this case, the roles and behaviors of white-collar attorneys. It follows with classifying aspects of the phenomenon into categories. Aspects for white-collar attorneys include themselves, their clients, attorney-client relationship, as well as situations involving rumors and facts about the alleged crime. Finally, stage three is to formulate a hypothesis of what causes the phenomenon to happen and why.

Other scholars also use the term "phenomenon," when trying to explain what is meant by theory. A phenomenon is an observable occurrence. It is the state of a thing or events that occur to a thing. A thing may change its state because of events. We try to explain or predict a phenomenon in an account (Weber, 2003).

In this chapter, a number of management and behavioral theories are applied to white-collar lawyers. Agency theory suggests that success is dependent on the principal-agent relationship; transaction cost theory argues that costs should be kept to a minimum; neutralization theory implies that both lawyer and client may consider the crime without guilt; attribution theory argues that external reasons are often preferred; resource theory suggests that strategic resources increases the likelihood of a mild sentence; and stages of growth theory implies that individuals and organizations move through stages over time in their unethical and criminal behavior.

Agency Theory with Principal and Agent

While the client can be defined as the principal who needs a lawyer's knowledge work, the lawyer can be defined as the agent carrying out knowledge work on behalf of the client. In this perspective, the relationship between client and lawyer can be studied in terms of agency theory with principal and agent. Agency theory has broadened the risk-sharing literature to include the agency problem that occurs when cooperating parties have different goals and division of labor. The cooperating parties are engaged in an agency relationship defined as a contract under which one or more persons [the principal(s) engage another person (agent) to perform some service on their behalf] delegate some decision-making authority to the agent (Jensen and Meckling, 1976). Agency theory describes the relationship between the two parties, using the concept of a contract.

According to Eisenhardt (1985), agency theory is concerned with resolving two problems that can occur in agency relationships. The first is the agency problem that arises when the desires or goals of the principal and agent conflict and it is difficult or expensive for the principal to verify what the agent is actually doing. Conflict of interest in a principal-agent relationship can lead to corrupt behavior, whether intentional or not. Conflict of interest can distort decision making on both sides (Banaji et al., 2003).

The second is the problem of risk sharing that arises when the principal and agent have different risk preferences. The first agency problem occurs when the two parties do not share productivity gains. The risk-sharing problem might be the result of different attitudes toward the use of new technologies, for example. Because the unit of analysis is the contract governing the relationship between the two parties, the focus of the theory is on determining the most efficient contract governing the principal-agent relationship given assumptions about people (e.g., self-interest, bounded rationality, risk aversion), organizations (e.g., goal conflict of members), and information (e.g., information is a commodity that can be purchased).

Garoupa (2007) applied agency theory to criminal organizations. He models the criminal firm as a family business with one principal and several agents. He has an illegal monopoly in mind where it is difficult to detect and punish the principal unless an agent is detected. Furthermore, it is assumed that agents work rather independently so that the likelihood of detection of one agent is fairly independent from that of another. An example of such agents is drug dealers in the street, with the principal being the local distributor. Another example would be agents as extortionists or blackmailers distributed across a city with the principal being the coordinator of their activities providing them with information or criminal know-how.

Gross (1978) discusses criminals as agents for a criminal organization in the following way:

> Although organizations are here held to be criminogenic and although courts no longer exhibit much hesitation in charging the organization itself with crime, organizations of course cannot themselves act—they must have agents who act for them. Who will the persons be who will act for organizations in their criminal behavior (65)?

In general, agency models view corruption and other kinds of financial crime as a consequence of the principal's inability to effectively prevent the agents from abusing their power for personal gain. The main reasons for this inability are the principal's lack of information about the agents' work, lack of effective checks and balances, and ineffective enforcement and punishment for criminal executives (Li and Ouyang, 2007).

Transaction Cost Theory of Cooperation

Attorney and client need to cooperate before, during, and after the trial. Transaction costs include both costs associated with conflicts and costs associated with misunderstandings (Wright, 2006):

> Transaction costs apply both to legitimate business and to illicit enterprises. They include the costs of conflicts and misunderstandings that lead to delays, to breakdowns and to other malfunctions. They can include such things as the costs of incentives, of ensuring co-ordination and the enforcement of regulations, rules or customs. In the case of a criminal organization, controlling transaction costs is necessary to keep it protected from betrayal and from prosecution. This includes the need to protect the organization from informers and from others (such as law enforcement agencies) who threaten its profits and stability. For such organizations, the use of violence and coercion is often the most effective way of reducing transaction costs (58).

Knowledge sharing between attorney and client can be a problem according to transaction cost theory. Transaction cost theory argues that if the costs of obtaining knowledge from others is too high, then it is more relevant to apply the knowledge one already has. Costs are measured in terms of time, effort, problems, communication, and other elements that make knowledge transfer difficult or even impossible.

There are several reasons why attorney-client knowledge sharing might be associated with high transaction costs. First, individuality in the legal profession implies that each professional is rather independent of colleagues as well as clients. By nature, law firms tend to foster a culture of individual practices. The individuality of lawyers complicates knowledge sharing. Lawyers and their departments within a law firm generally consider themselves—or want to consider themselves— self-employed. This is reflected in the client relationship, where the client is considered a source of information and not as a resource to find an optimal solution.

Another reason why knowledge sharing might be associated with high transaction costs is the relative power of a defense counsel, which may diminish if the client is allowed to learn the same kind of skills and gain the same kind of insights. Among professionals, power is part of their skills as knowledge, and skills offer the lawyer power. If too much knowledge is shared, then transaction costs may emerge in the form of criticism from the client. There are many more reasons why knowledge sharing is associated with high transaction costs. As a result of the individualistic nature of the legal profession, there is a lack of sufficient trust and loyalty between attorney and client in order to accommodate effective knowledge transfer. Often, knowledge workers need to know each other to trust each other.

Neutralization Theory about Guilt

Even if the defense lawyer thinks his client is guilty, it can make sense to help the client into a state of mind of not feeling guilt. Guilt is a feeling that can be reduced or eliminated by applying neutralization techniques (Stadler and Benson, 2012). Defense lawyers may try to convince clients of less guilt than previously perceived. Prosecuted white-collar criminals will behave more professionally in court if they do not feel too much guilt.

Criminals apply techniques to make them feel they have done nothing wrong. These techniques are called neutralization techniques, because the feeling of guilt is neutralized. Neutralization theory is the umbrella for all these techniques. In their original formulation of neutralization theory, Sykes and Matza (1957) proposed five techniques of neutralization: denial of responsibility, denial of injury, denial of the victim, condemnation of the condemners, and appeal to higher loyalties. Later, other researchers added the metaphor of the ledger and a technique named the defense of necessity.

The following neutralization techniques are included in neutralization theory today.

Denial of responsibility. The offender here claims that one or more of the conditions of responsible agency were not met. The person committing a deviant act defines himself as lacking responsibility for his actions. In this technique, the person rationalizes that the action in question is beyond his control. The offender views himself as a billiard ball, helplessly propelled through different situations.

Denial of injury. The offender seeks to minimize or deny the harm done. Denial of injury involves justifying an action by minimizing the harm it causes. The misbehavior is not really serious because no party suffers directly as a result of it.

Denial of victim. The offender acknowledges the injury but claims that the victim is unworthy of concern. Any blame for illegal actions are not justified because the violated party deserves whatever injury they receive.

Condemnation of the condemners. The offender tries to accuse his critics of questionable motives for criticizing him. According to this technique, actions are neutralized by blaming those who are the target of the action. The offender deflects moral condemnation to those ridiculing corporations by pointing out that they engage in similar immoral behavior.

Appeal to higher loyalties. The offender denies the act was motivated by self-interest, claiming that it was instead done out of obedience to some moral obligation. This technique is employed by those who feel they are in a dilemma that must be resolved at the cost of violating a law or policy. In an organizational context, an employee may appeal to organizational values or hierarchies. For example, an employee could argue that she must violate a policy in order to get her work done.

Normality of action. The offender argues that everyone else is doing it, thus he has done nothing wrong.

Claim to entitlement. The offender claims she was within her rights to do what she did, maybe because of a very stressful situation or because of some misdeed perpetrated by the victim. This is defense of necessity, which is based on the justification that if the rule-breaking is viewed as necessary, one should not feel guilty when committing the action.

Legal mistake. The offender argues the law is wrong, and what he did should indeed not be illegal. One may break the law because the law is unreasonable.

Acceptable mistake. The offender argues that what she did is acceptable given the situation and given her position. The person feels she has been doing so much good for the organization, that she should be excused for more wrongdoings than other people and that her crime is a minor matter that should be ignored. This is in line with the metaphor of the ledger, which uses the idea of compensating bad acts with good acts. That is, an individual believes that she has previously performed a number of good acts and has gained a surplus of good will, and as a result of this, can afford to do some bad actions. Executives in corporate environments neutralize their actions through the metaphor of the ledger by rationalizing that their overall past good behavior justifies occasional rule-breaking.

Dilemma tradeoff. The offender argues there was a dilemma for him where he made a reasonable tradeoff before committing the act. Tradeoff between many interests resulted in the offense. Dilemma represents a state of mind where it is not obvious what action is right and what is wrong. For example, the offense might be carried out to prevent a more serious offense to happen.

Justifications are socially constructed accounts that individuals who engage in criminal acts adopt to legitimize their behavior. Justifications are beliefs that counteract negative interpretations by articulating why the acts are excusable exceptions to the norms.

Attribution Theory for Explanations

In addition to establishing the facts and identifying relevant laws for white-collar crime, behavioral explanations in terms of motives are of importance in the court. Motives are reasons for actions. If the motive is personal greed, it is not so good. If the motive is environmental pressure or even necessity, then it is better. Motives in terms of causal relationships may be subject to interpretation by lawyer and client. Attribution theory can help us understand what is going on here.

Attribution theory is concerned with how one chooses explanatory factors for a phenomenon. Usually a distinction is made between internal and external explanatory factors. If a criminal act occurs, then the act can be explained by internal factors that are attributed to the criminal or by external factors that are attributed to the environment and the situation.

Attribution theory is about identifying causality based on internal and external circumstances (Eberly et al., 2011):

> Identifying the locus of causality has been at the core of attribution theory since its inception and has generated an extensive research stream in the field of organizational behavior. But the question emerges whether the "internal" and "external" categories capture the entire conceptual space of this phenomenon (731).

Based on this argument, Eberly et al. suggest there is a third category in addition to internal explanation and external explanation, which is labeled relational explanation. These three categories of attributes can be explored to find causal explanations regarding how persons react in criminal situations.

Attribution theory is a part of social psychology that studies how humans spontaneously place reasons, guilt, and responsibility in situations that occur. The fundamental attribution error is a term used for an overemphasis on personality rather than situational factors to explain behavior.

Conspiracy Theory of External Causes

One of the most widely held theories of organized crime today in the United States is known as the "alien conspiracy theory." This theory blames outsiders and outside influences for the prevalence of organized crime in society. Over the years, unsavory images, such as well-dressed men of foreign descent standing in shadows with machine guns and living by codes of silence, have become associated with this theory. The alien conspiracy theory posits that organized crime (the Mafia) gained prominence during the 1860s in Sicily and that Sicilian immigrants are responsible for the foundations of U.S. organized crime, which is made up of 25 or so Italian-dominated crime families (Lyman and Potter, 2007).

In line with this thinking, a lawyer and/or a client may introduce a conspiracy theory about the police, the prosecution, the court, the prison, and all other organizations involved in criminal handling. It can be argued that prestige has entered the thinking of crime investigators, that the court wants to set an example, and that everyone is out to get the white-collar suspect, including the media. Both the defense lawyer and the client might be convinced—or at least express—that there is a larger conspiracy surrounding and driving the white-collar crime case.

Lyman and Potter (2007) discuss this theory in the following way:

> Although some skeptics insist that the alien conspiracy theory was born out of hysteria incited by the media, it has received considerable support over the years from federal law enforcement organizations, public officials, and some researchers. It has been argued, however, that federal law enforcement organizations have self-serving reasons to promulgate this theory: It explains their inability to eliminate organized crime, it disguises the role of political and business corruption in organized crime, and it provides fertile ground for new resources, powers, and bureaucratic expansion (60).

Lombardo (2002) has challenged the alien conspiracy theory as an explanation of the origin of organized crime in America, as he reviewed the history of Black Hand (organized crime group) activity in Chicago in the early twentieth century, arguing that the development of Black Hand extortion was not related to the emergence of the Sicilian Mafia, but rather to the social structure of American society.

Resource-Based Theory for Knowledge Access

White-collar criminals tend to have access to more resources than street criminals. Resources—including knowledge, money, network, and alliances—enable a more favorable process and verdict. The defense lawyer is an important resource to the defendant. According to the resource-based theory, performance differences in court cases can be attributed to the variance in the defendant's resources and capabilities. Knowledge that is valuable, unique, inimitable, combinable, irreplaceable, and exploitable can provide the basis for attorney's competitive advantages. The essence of the resource-based theory of the defense lies in its emphasis on the internal resources—here, knowledge—available to the defense, rather than on the external opportunities and threats dictated by the prosecution and the court.

The resource-based view posits that competitiveness comes from unique bundles of tangible and intangible assets that are valuable, rare, imperfectly imitable, irreplaceable, combinable, and sustainable.

Stages of Growth Theory for Relationship

The powerful concept of stages of growth is extremely important in management research. To capture this concept, we introduce stages of growth modeling and present elements of a growth stage theory exemplified with the case of lawyer-client relationships.

We propose that a relationship may change over time due to interactions and challenges. The change occurs in discrete stages with their own unique characteristics.

Researchers have struggled for decades to develop stages of growth models that are both theoretically founded and empirically validated. However, stages of growth models have the potential of creating new knowledge and insights into organizational phenomena. Such models represent theory-building tools that conceptualize evolution over time in a variety of areas. For researchers, a stage model represents a theory to be explored and empirically validated. For practitioners, a stage model represents a picture of evolution, where the current stage can be understood in terms of history and future.

A model of client-lawyer relationships is presented below in terms of three stages. The stages are resource stage, agent stage, and partner stage, respectively, as illustrated in Figure 7.1.

In her 2007 article "The Devil Made Me Do It: Business Partners in Crime," Beare explains why and how lawyers commit illegal

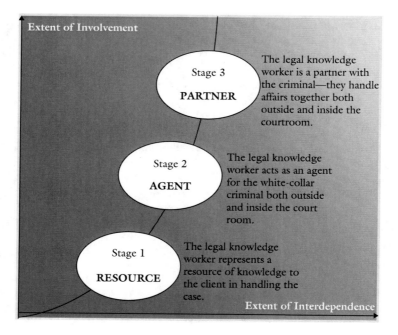

Figure 7.1 Stages of lawyer involvement in client affairs

actions together with criminals at the partner stage. By following the money trail, she writes about different situations such as "clean and dirty money in, clean and dirty money out," "dirty money in, clean money out," and "dirty money in, dirty (laundered) money out".

Table 7.1 Theories to provide insights into the role of white-collar lawyers

Theory	Characteristics	Yes/No	Explanation
Agency Theory Principal= Criminal Agent= Lawyer Opportunistic behavior?	The principal is unable to know what the agent is doing. The agent is unable to know what the principal is doing. Principal and agent are in a state of goal conflict. Principal and agent have different degrees of risk willingness.		
Transaction Cost Theory Huge costs of cooperation?	Client crime case is quite unusual and rare. Client has a hard time communicating with lawyer. Lawyer has a hard time communicating with client.		
Neutralization Theory Defendant feels not guilty?	Lawyer thinks client is not guilty because there is no injury, no victim, no responsibility etc.		
Attribution Theory External explanatory factors?	Lawyer argues external factors—for which the client is not responsible—are reasons for the crime.		
Conspiracy Theory External conspiracy against client?	Lawyer argues that the police and prosecutor have decided to win and defeat the white-collar defender at all costs. Lawyer argues there is substantial prestige invested in the case on the prosecution side.		
Resource Theory Better access to a fair trial?	Lawyer pre-presents the case in the media. Lawyer is extra paid by client. Lawyer knowledge is unique, irreplaceable, inimitable exploitable, valuable, nontransferrable, and combinable.		
Growth Theory At what stage is the relationship?	Lawyer is a resource to the client. Lawyer is an agent for the client. Lawyer is a partner with the client.		

Comparison of Theoretical Perspectives

Theories presented above can be summarized in the table that follows. For each theory, a few statements typically indicating theory core are listed in the second column. The table can be applied to evaluate one specific white-collar lawyer at a time. Evaluation is carried out by answering yes or no to each statement and then arguing the case for yes or no in the column for explanation.

8

Empirical Study of White-Collar Lawyers

Several options exist to identify a substantial sample of white-collar criminals and to collect relevant information about each criminal and his or her lawyer. However, in a small country like Norway with a population of only five million people, there are limits to available sample size. One option would be to study court cases involving white-collar crime and criminals. A challenge in that case would be to identify the relevant laws and sentences that cover this book's definition not only of white-collar crime, but also the required characteristics of white-collar criminals.

Another available option is to study newspaper articles in which the journalists already have conducted some kind of selection of higher class, white-collar individuals convicted in court because of financial crime. An advantage of this approach is that the cases are publicly known, which makes it easier to identify cases by individual white-collar names. The selective and otherwise filtered information in newspapers might be a problem in other kinds of studies but is considered acceptable in this study. Therefore, the latter option was chosen in this research.

Sample of Lawyers

Our sample has the following characteristics as applied by newspapers when presenting news: famous individuals, famous companies, surprising stories, important events, substantial consequences, matters of principle, and significant public interest. The sample consists of high-profile and large-yield offenses. This is in line with research by Schnatterly (2003), who searched the *Wall Street Journal* for several years in her study of white-collar crime that was published in the *Strategic Management Journal*.

The two main financial newspapers in Norway are *Dagens Næringsliv* and *Finansavisen*, both of which are conservative-leaning business newspapers. In addition, the business-friendly national daily newspaper, *Aftenposten*, regularly reports news of white-collar criminals. Left-wing newspapers such as *Klassekampen* very seldom cover specific white-collar criminal cases, although they generally report on white-collar crime. It is important to understand the agenda setting and framing functions of the media, perhaps the two most important schemes in journalism, media, and communication studies, and clearly relevant as the theme and focus of this article.

Dagens Næringsliv, Finansavisen, and *Aftenposten* were studied on a daily basis from 2009 to 2012 to identify white-collar criminals. A total of 329 convicted white-collar criminals were reported during those years. A criminal was defined as white-collar if the person satisfied the general criteria mentioned previously in this chapter, and if the person was sentenced in court to imprisonment. It was possible to identify names of attorneys for 277 convicts, which represent 84 percent of the total sample.

It is important to keep in mind that our selection of defense lawyers is based on newspaper accounts of white-collar crime, not the distribution of white-collar crime in society, because that is not what is being measured. Using a newspaper sample is different from the population of white-collar crime cases. We argue that a newspaper account is one of the characteristics of white-collar crime as defined previously. Therefore, news reports are relevant reflections of knowledge about white-collar crime.

As suggested by Barak (2007), newsmaking criminology refers to the conscious efforts and activities of criminologists to interpret, influence, or shape the representation of newsworthy items about crime and justice. Newsmaking criminology as a perspective on the theory, practice, and representation of crime and justice is an important approach for understanding white-collar crime. However, Barak's work focused on how the media constructs images of crime.

In his research, the media is used as a source of potentially objective information: factual information in terms of quantitative numbers is collected from newspaper accounts.

We make no distinction between prison and jail in this study. A prison or jail in Norway is a place in which people are physically confined and deprived of a range of personal freedoms. Imprisonment is a legal penalty that is imposed by the state for commission of a crime judged in court. In the United States, the difference between jail and prison is primarily a function of imprisonment length, where the use of prison over jail implies a more serious punishment.

Our operational definition of white-collar crime restricts the sample to those who receive jail time as punishment. This restriction excludes cases of fines as penal response, which is quite common. This sample restriction enables us to only study serious white-collar crime cases. Our intention is not to identify white-collar crime in reference to the law, but mainly with respect to the reporting of these offenses resulting in imprisonment. If the sample would be selected as references by the law, then a number of offenses would be defined in noncriminal statutes. Noncriminal statutes cannot, by their definition, result in jail time, only in civil remedies. Thus, by taking this view, we have essentially omitted most white-collar crime cases of fines from our study, since their severity is of a minor extent.

Research articles suggest that only the most serious white-collar crime offenders end up in prison. For this study, it was considered sufficient that the person was sentenced in one court, even if the person represented a recent case that still had appeals pending for higher courts. A sentence was defined as a jail sentence.

The following analysis is limited to imprisoned white-collar offenders and their attorneys. Since our research is based on newspaper articles written by journalists, the reliability and completeness of such a source is a challenge in social research. However, most cases were presented in several newspapers over several days, weeks, or even months, enabling this research to correct erroneous initial facts as more information became available. Additionally, court documents were obtained whenever there was doubt about the reliability of a single newspaper report that could not be confirmed by other media. This happened in one-third of the reported cases.

It must be noted that there are, of course, disadvantages in using newspapers as data sources. Research articles suggest that the media present a distorted image of crime by focusing on violent, sensational events that are atypical of crime in society. These researchers argue that the media is neglecting coverage of corporate offenses and that they disproportionately focus on conventional crime while neglecting the impact of corporate misbehavior. This line of reasoning does not only acknowledge possible biases in our research, but it can also be understood as an argument for our research design, where an important characteristic of our sample is that the white-collar crime cases are prominent in the media.

Nevertheless, some types of corporate crime—probably those that are more typical—maybe still go unreported than other types of corporate crime. For instance, the media may be biased against small corporate offenses, preferring larger, more sensational cases.

Two methodological issues have to be kept in mind because of our decision to use newspapers as sources:

- *Bias because of press coverage.* Financial crime committed by white-collar criminals is only exposed in the press to the extent that the crimes and the criminals are sensational and possibly revealed and discovered by the press itself. Therefore, no claim is made that the sample is representative of white-collar criminals in general. Rather, there is a bias toward white-collar criminals that, for some reason, are of special interest to journalists and newspapers that cover their story. Therefore, the attribute of news coverage is explicitly added to the list of attributes for white-collar criminals, including items such as position of trust, network, and opportunity. White-collar crimes are committed by people at all levels of the social structure—all they need is the opportunity and mindset. Looking at only those reported in the newspapers, the high visibility white-collar crimes certainly bias the results toward people at the higher social level.
- *Data errors in press coverage.* Newspaper articles tend to have some errors in them. There may be factual errors, such as offender name, offender age, sentence, crime type, and crime year. Furthermore, there may be a disproportionate focus on the sensational aspects of both criminal and crime. Everyone who has ever read about himself or herself in the newspaper will know that there are errors or wrong impressions in the presentation. To minimize this source of error, several newspaper stories of the same case were read and cited based on investigative research. Furthermore, court sentences were obtained in most of the cases to check both factual and story elements concerning both criminal and crime.

However, an argument in favor of media as source of information is integrity measurement by Transparency International. In 2012, Renå applied the National Integrity System (NIS) for Transparency International to analyze and quantify the extent of integrity in Norwegian institutions in society. At the top of the list of pillars' in the country's governance system, both in terms of their internal corruption risks and their contribution to fighting corruption in society at large, we find the media in Norway. The pillars analyzed in a NIS include: legislative branch of government, executive branch of government, judiciary, public sector, law enforcement, electoral management body, ombudsman, audit institution, anticorruption agencies, political parties, civil society, business, and media. With a score of 96 percent, media achieved top ranking in Norway. Reasons for a high media score include judicial framework enabling an independent press, media diversity, transparency in media activities, accountability of editors, and independence of journalists.

It must be noted that journalists in Norway enjoy respectability because of their integrity and seriousness. Very few newspapers, if any, are engaged in reporting undocumented, sensational stories. In fact, during our research into financial crime by white-collar criminals, we have not found one such newspaper in Norway. Some journalists in the Norwegian financial press have developed sophisticated skills in digging for criminal cases, where they apply robust and transparent methodologies. Every year in Norway, a prestigious prize, the SKUP award, is given to the journalist(s) who has (have) conducted an investigation and reported news in a professional way. The prize is awarded by the Norwegian Foundation for a Free and Investigative Press to someone who both found and reported a good story in a respectable and professional way.

A newspaper sample might suffer from severe selection biases that have to be taken into account when studying research results:

- Newspaper articles will disproportionately discuss more serious cases, which are the crimes with longer sentences, giving a bias toward crimes with long sentences.
- Selecting cases with sentences instead of fines will also produce cases with longer sentences and thus give skewed distribution to the data.
- The average dollar amount involved in each crime will be higher since newspaper articles generally focus on more serious crimes.
- Most crimes were committed by a group as again, newspaper articles are more likely to discuss these cases because conspiracies are more newsworthy than other individual crimes.

- A significant number of criminals in high management positions will be present in the sample, again, because newspapers are more likely to discuss crime committed by higher-level employees.
- The size of the company in terms of turnover and employees will be at the higher end, and the company will tend to be profitable, since crime against more successful companies is more likely to be newsworthy.

The danger of media as an information source for research into white-collar crime has been wisely emphasized by several scholars. For example, Goldstraw-White (2012) warns that journalist research is often biased, aimed at producing a good story rather than a factual report, and tends to highlight particular types of offenders, such as those regarded as famous. However, since being famous or becoming famous is part of our definition, this bias is acceptable for the current research. Goldstraw-White, in her research, applied a small convenience sample of white-collar criminals in prison who were interviewed about their offending behavior.

Newspaper articles are suitable for content analysis, which is the research method applied in the following. This can tell us a lot about how media organizations frame and depict white-collar crime, but it cannot be used as a direct reflection of the real number or nature of white-collar crime in Norway. It has value in its ability to examine the social construction of white-collar criminality in Norway's financial media.

Characteristics of Lawyers

Out of 277 convicted white-collar criminals, 238 convicts were defended by a male lawyer and 39 by a female lawyer. Among 277 white-collar convicts, there were 253 men and 24 women. An emerging question is whether men defend men and women defend women. This was not the case, as 20 women were defended by men, and 4 women by women. This reflects the general gender distribution and cannot tell anything about gender preference in attorney selection. While 16.7 percent of the women selected a female lawyer, 13.8 percent of the men selected a female lawyer as well. In total, women represent 14.1 percent of the lawyers and 9 percent of the convicted criminals.

There are a total of 172 lawyers in the sample, which implies that each lawyer defended 1.6 criminals on average. The lawyer with most clients defended 20 convicts in the sample.

Average age of lawyers was 51 years old, while average age of criminals was 48. The youngest lawyer was 26 years, while the oldest was 83. Average taxable income was $200,000 US (1,253,000 Norwegian kroner), and the best earning attorney had an income of $2 million.

Correlation analysis indicates a positive relation between the number of white-collar crime clients and lawyer taxable income. Furthermore, older lawyers have higher incomes. No relationship was found between number of clients and age of lawyer.

Some lawyers are more famous than others. How well-known a lawyer is to potential clients and to the general public might be measured in terms of media coverage. Financial newspapers represent a relevant source of fame for white-collar people. The largest Norwegian financial newspaper, *Dagens Næringsliv*, was searched for hits on their website. The most famous lawyer achieved 219 hits, followed by the second most famous lawyer with 112 hits on the newspaper's website.

This fame factor in terms of website hits was correlated with other variables for the lawyers. A significant and positive relationship emerged between fame factor and number of clients, as well as between fame factor and lawyer income. Results are listed in Table 8.1.

Furthermore, there is significant correlation between income and clients, as well as income and age. In the first two columns, average values and standard deviations are listed. The average number of white-collar clients for each white-collar lawyer in the sample over a three-year period is 1.6 criminals, with a standard deviation of 1.8 criminals.

Table 8.1 Correlation analysis for white-collar crime lawyers (statistical significance is measured in terms of probability of possible mistake, where mistake is .05 at * and .01 at **)

	Average	Deviation	Clients	b	Income	b
Clients	1.6	1.8	1	−.059	.576**	.947**
Age	51.3	11.3		1	.185**	.002
Income	1.3	1.4			1	.608**
Fame	8.1	24.0				1

White-collar criminals commit their crimes in terms of a money amount. The amount of money varies from case to case, where the average in the sample is $8 million (51 million Norwegian kroner). The largest sum of money in a single case was $200 million in a bank fraud by a large company. An interesting issue is whether characteristics of lawyers can somehow predict money amount and jail sentence. Correlation analysis indicates that significant relationships exist between crime amount and lawyer fame (.141*), lawyer income (.234**) and lawyer age (.145**). There is no significant correlation between number of clients and crime amount. Significance is measured in terms of probability, where ** means .01 significance and * means .05 significance in statistical terms.

White-collar criminals in the database were convicted to prison sentences. An average jail sentence for 277 convicted white-collar criminals was 2.3 years. An interesting issue is whether characteristics of attorneys in any way might predict sentence length. Potential predictors include number of clients, lawyer age, lawyer income, and lawyer fame. Correlation analysis indicates no such relationships.

When disregarding characteristics of defense lawyers, the most important predictor of a jail sentence for white-collar criminals is the crime's dollar amount. With a significant and positive correlation coefficient (.249**), imprisonment increases as crime's dollar amount grows in the sample.

So far, it is established that prison sentence becomes more severe with a larger crime amount, and the crime amount is larger when a famous lawyer is defending the case. When these two factors are combined with the number of clients, some interesting results emerge from regression analysis:

- A larger amount of money in the crime is positively related to a longer jail sentence.
- A defense lawyer with more fame is positively related to a shorter jail sentence.
- A higher number of clients are positively related to a longer jail sentence.

These regression results are significant, and taken together, amount, fame, and clients can predict variation in prison sentence, as listed in Table 8.2.

Table 8.2 Regression analysis with jail sentence as dependent variable

	Slope	T-value	Significance
Number of white-collar clients	0.183	2.552	.011
Website hits for lawyer fame	−0.15	−2.516	.012
Amount of money involved in crime	0.03	4.683	.000

All three factors in the table are significant from a statistical point of view ($p < .05$). The minus sign in front of fame indicates that fame is related to shorter jail sentence for the client.

Entrepreneurial Characteristics

In the study just discussed, entrepreneurial characteristics in lawyers representing white-collar criminals were determined, based on the Norwegian context. Statistical analysis indicates that the higher the amount of money involved in a white-collar crime, the longer the jail sentence imposed. Moreover, it demonstrates that hiring a defense lawyer with a reputation (a high level of fame) is positively related to a shorter jail sentence, whereas hiring a defense lawyer with numerous clients results in the client receiving a longer jail sentence. Using agency theory, we argue that white-collar defense agents exhibit entrepreneurial characteristics in their everyday working practices.

The role of the white-collar defense agent is to act entrepreneurially and engage in damage limitation to author a plausible defense based on their legal experience and knowledge with the intention of extracting the client from a predicament. This contrasts sharply with Osiel's (1990) view of the moral ideal of legal service, but fits his view of the lawyer-client relationship as being loyalty to the client. We make it clear here we are talking about lawyers who serve their client "zealously within the bounds of the law" (Atkins, 1995) and not so-called "gangland" lawyers who act criminally outside the law (Morton, 2013). In an entrepreneurial culture, a law firm is both conscience and continuity (Gupta, 2005), but the legal system operates competitively on a winner-takes-all basis.

When prosecuted in court, white-collar criminals are defended by specialist lawyers. Law is at once increasingly broad and increasingly specialized (Miller et al., 2012). This makes legal knowledge an entrepreneurial endeavor. An analysis of the entrepreneurial characteristics of lawyers adds an important insight to our understanding of the nuances of white-collar crime. The notion of the lawyer as entrepreneur and of the entrepreneurial nature of practicing law is an emerging one (Osiel, Gupta, Miller et al.). Again, entrepreneurial characteristics are at play. It is all about coming up with different, novel approaches to solving the problem. This is the basis of creative thinking in business, and in many ways the white-collar criminals who know they are guilty and who are looking for a creative solution to a business problem have to trust the lawyer to come up with a successful approach to solving their problems.

There is pressure on lawyers to perform consistently at a high level and to get results. In this respect the lawyer as entrepreneur is similar to the philosopher Thomas Hobbes's detective-entrepreneur in that "working, lurking, and getting results" is their primary objective (Hobbs, 1989). In addition, the lawyer enjoys attorney-client privilege, which when combined with confidentiality, means that a lawyer does not have to prove innocence, merely introduce reasonable doubt. Clearly there is scope for a blurring of boundaries to occur particularly between truth and the hypothetical.

In agency theory, the client can be defined as the principal who needs a lawyer's knowledge work; the lawyer can be defined as the agent carrying out knowledge work on behalf of the client. In this perspective, the relationship between client and lawyer can be studied in terms of agency theory with principal and agent. Agency theory describes the relationship between the two parties using the concept of a contract (Jensen and Meckling, 1976).

First-Time Offenders

When white-collar criminals appear before their sentencing judges, they can correctly claim to be first-time offenders. They are wealthy, highly educated, and socially connected. They are elite individuals, according to the description and attitudes of white-collar criminals as suggested by Sutherland (1940, 1949, 1983). They may well also belong to clubs and fraternal societies.

Therefore, very few white-collar criminals seem to be put on trial, and even fewer higher-class criminals are sentenced to imprisonment. If they are, they go to a type of prison that is said to be a "country-club" type. This is in contrast to most other financial crime sentences, where the criminals who appear in the justice system are typically not wealthy, highly educated, or socially connected. White-collar criminals are not entrenched in traditional criminal lifestyles as are common street criminals. Some of them belong to the elite in society and are typically individuals who either own or are employed by legitimate organizations.

What Podgor (2007) found to be the most interesting aspect of Sutherland's work is that a scholar needed to proclaim that crimes of the upper socioeconomic class were, in fact, crimes that should be prosecuted. It is apparent that prior to the coining of the term "white-collar crime," wealth and power allowed some persons to escape criminal liability. These individuals were characterized by their high economic and/or social status, the high levels of trust among their communities, and the fact that their criminal acts were made possible by their legitimate employment, special knowledge, or corporate ownership.

Why would white-collar crime lawyers be different from other specialist lawyers? Those who can afford it will always hire the best lawyers to defend or argue their case. The rich and powerful will always have better access to justice because they can pay for the services of lawyers who have expertise on the case at issue and are being paid for the hours they render versus a public defense attorney who does not have the time to study rigidly or devote his or her time to the case. Examples are divorce cases in the US, the UK, or Italy, where parties hire the best divorce lawyers. It could also be that lawyers employed in the public sector are often not as brilliant as their counterparts. Top law firms often hire top law graduates, and those who cannot make it in the profession, may end up outside the firms.

Access to justice depends on many factors, including a defense lawyer who is willing to select the case. Trautner (2011) studied what shapes lawyers' case selections. She found that previous studies suggest that lawyers use a simple risk/return formula to make such decisions. She argues, however, that legal environments also shape lawyers' decisions. Analysis of in-depth interviews with lawyers across four states demonstrates that lawyers make different decisions about cases in different legal environments. Lawyers in states without tort reform emphasized the importance of how likeable a client may be to a potential jury, whereas lawyers in states with tort reform instead focus on the defendant's liability. These differences impact the extent of access to justice.

Anderson and Heaton (2012) studied how much difference the lawyer makes. Although their study was concerned with murder cases, it is nevertheless interesting and relevant. One in five indigent murder defendants in Philadelphia is randomly assigned representation by public defenders, while the remainder receive court-appointed private attorneys. The study exploited this random assignment to measure how defense counsel affects murder case outcomes. Compared to appointed counsel, public defenders in Philadelphia reduce their clients' murder conviction rate by 19 percent and lower the probability that their clients receive a life sentence by 62 percent. Public defenders reduce overall expected time served in prison by 24 percent. Furthermore, the study shows no difference in the overall number of charges of which defendants are found guilty. When the study applied methods used in past studies of the effect of counsel that did not use random assignment, it obtained far more modest estimated impacts, which suggests defendant sorting is an important confounder affecting past research.

To understand possible explanations for the disparity in outcomes, Anderson and Heaton interviewed judges, public defenders, and attorneys who took appointments. Interviewees identified a variety of institutional factors in Philadelphia that decreased the likelihood that appointed counsel would prepare cases as well as the public defenders. The vast difference in outcomes for defendants assigned different counsel types raises important questions about the adequacy and fairness of the criminal justice system.

White-collar crime lawyers are different from other specialist lawyers because of the knowledge gap, the resource gap, and the uncertainty surrounding whether an act represents a crime that has actually been committed. Corporate financial crime cases have a tendency to be associated with great uncertainty in terms of know-what, know-how, and know-why. This uncertainty makes judges—who are not necessarily familiar with international business operations—uncertain whether a crime has been committed at all. A situation is then created in court where it is very much up to defense lawyers to present the case in such a manner that it seems to be outside punishable conditions. Defense lawyers can present causes and links in the case as business evidence for pleading not guilty, where judges have a hard time following the business lines, business actors, and consequences in relation to Norwegian law.

Based on exploratory research, this study revealed some interesting insights into potential links between lawyers and their clients in a Norwegian context. From a statistical point of view, the higher the amount of money involved in the crime, the longer the jail sentence. Also, a defense lawyer with more fame is more likely to get a result in terms of a shorter jail sentence for the client. Conversely, choosing a defense lawyer with numerous clients is more likely to result in clients receiving a longer jail sentence. These are interesting preliminary results. In future research concerning lawyer-client relationships, it will be useful to examine common lines of defense run by such solicitors, and how these rely on exploiting techniques of neutralization (Gottschalk and Smith, 2011). However, it is apparent that white-collar defense agents are from the same privileged class as their white-collar business clients, and that they can use their standing, status, and entrepreneurial strategies to good effect in getting a result for their clients.

Lawyers in Serious Cases

Our sample of 277 white-collar defense cases is too long to be listed in a meaningful way. However, parts of the list may be derived based on different criteria. The following list in Table 8.3 contains the most serious cases in terms of imprisonment.

The first on the list is attorney Bjørn Stordrange at law firm Steenstrup Stordrange, which is one of the largest law firms in Norway, with more than fifty partners and two hundred employees. Bjørn Stordrange was born in 1956. His law degree and his doctoral degree are both from the University of Oslo. Stordrange's taxable income in 2009 was 12 million Norwegian kroner, which is about $ 2 million US. This amount is far above the average of white-collar defense lawyers in Norway because Stordrange is one of two senior partners in the firm, where his name is part of the firm name of Steenstrup Stordrange.

On their website www.steenstrup.no, Steenstrup Stordrange presents firm attorneys in this way:

> Steenstrup Stordrange is one of the country's largest law firms with offices in Norway's most important business centres and industrial zones. Employee career development is prioritised at our law firm. We hire ambitious and highly competent attorneys. Our success depends on our ability to attract, develop and keep hold of the most talented professionals. Steenstrup Stordrange is a dynamic company with a structured

Table 8.3 Top white-collar crime cases in terms of years in prison

#	Case	Person	Age	Prison	Defense Lawyer	Law Firm
1	Acta	Ingebrigtsen, Fred	48	9	Stordrange, Bjørn	Steenstrup Stordrange
2	Finance Credit	Kristoffersen, Trond	52	9	Brosveet, Anders	Elden
3	Eltek	Angelil, Alain	69	8	Reiss-Andersen, B.	Reiss-Andersen
4	Vannverk	Henriksen, Ivar Thorer	72	8	Fougner, Else Bugge	Hjort
5	Plastic Fantastic	Holst-Cappelen, Philip	21	8	Ihlebæk, Oscar	Ihlebæk
6	Drosjesvindel	Amundsen, Henry	57	7	Feydt, Fridtjov	Feydt Hamborgstrøm
7	Undervisnings-bygg	Murud, Frank	51	7	Brosveet, Anders	Elden
8	Finance Credit	Stensrud, Torgeir	59	7	Stabell, Harald	Stabell
9	Lucia	Ezazi, Sharok	38	6.5	Hessen, Anita	Hessen
10	Dekoder	Alsaedi, Abdul Hadi	44	6	Iversen, Vidar Lind	Iversen
11	Klimakvote	Andresen, Kenneth	33	6	Vordahl, Nils Jørgen	Aurlien Vordahl
12	Acta	Nilsen, Kåre	43	6	Torstrup, Odd-Rune	Torstrup
13	Acta	Lunde, Lars Audun	47	6	Helljesen, Atle	Legal
14	Mohr	Mohr, Christian	55	6	Brosveet, Anders	Elden
15	Røde Kors	Nielsen, Peter Aksel	67	6	Holden, Arild	Elden
16	Stål	Schmitz, Wolfgang	71	6	Aas, Arne Gunnar	Hjort
17	Fortuna	Stärk-Johansen, Knut	54	6	Veum, Johnny	Andenæs Aaløkken
18	Fortuna	Børresen, Ole	57	6	Andreassen, Pål	Andreassen
19	Fortuna	Trollebø, Frode	56	6	Stordrange, Bjørn	Steenstrup Stordrange
20	Tromsdal	Tromsdal, Christer	36	6	Skjerdal, Karl	Hjort

programme for employee competence development. This process focuses on professional development, essential markets and providing a high level of quality to our customers. We support our employees in their career development and evaluate their professional progress based on how they develop as individuals and how they contribute to the professional development of fellow employees. Our recruitment programme emphasises legal competence, understanding of commercial matters and communication and network building skills.

How do we keep talented people? Our colleagues tell us that they enjoy their work. It is that easy and that difficult. We think the answer lies in the opportunity to work in-depth and across a wide range of fields and the possibility of working with experienced lawyers who know their craft—within a youthful, informal and enjoyable environment.

The second on the list is defense attorney Anders Brosveet at law firm Elden. Brosveet was born in 1969 and made 2.8 million NOK (about $450,000 US) in 2009. He is general manager of the law firm Elden. He has experience and assignments in procedure and criminal law. He has served as defense counsel in a number of the most comprehensive economic criminal cases in Norway over the last 10 years, and therefore has broad experience in handling litigation, contract, and corporate law.

The law firm Elden is a medium-sized law firm in Norway. It is a procedural law firm consisting of 46 employees, including 31 attorneys. Four of the attorneys are admitted to the Norwegian Supreme Court, and one attorney has additional qualifications as MBA (Master of Business Administration). In essence, the Elden law firm offers legal services related to criminal cases and disputes/litigation in civil cases. Within the criminal justice field, they are one of the country's largest law firms. The firm is headquartered in Oslo, but handles matters throughout the country.

The third lawyer on the list is Berit Reiss-Andersen. She runs her own law firm, Reiss-Andersen & Co., with seven lawyers and a secretary. It is a small law firm that provides legal assistance to Norwegian and foreign clients in both civil law and criminal law.

Ranking of Defense Lawyers

Lawyers defending clients in financial crime cases rank each other on an annual basis and publish results in the Norwegian financial newspaper *Finansavisen*. Attorney Erling Lyngtveit is ranked first, followed by John Christian Elden, Erik Keiserud, Bjørn Stordrange, and Anders Brosveet, as listed in Table 8.4.

Second column in the table lists fame, where fame is measured in the number of hits on business newspaper website *Dagens Næringsliv* (*Dn.no*). There we find Elden first, followed by Andenæs and Stordrange. Third column shows ranking in terms of the number of white-collar criminals in the database defended by that particular

Table 8.4 Ranking of lawyers depending on colleagues, fame, cases, and income (For lawyers Keiserud and Schiøtz there were no cases, but if there were, they would be third on the income list; instead Fougner is third on the income list, and the second on the income list of lawyers is not a white-collar defense lawyer)

White-collar defense lawyers in Norway	Ranking by colleagues (Finansavisen)	Ranking by business fame (Dn.no)	Ranking by cases (Database)	Ranking by income in 2009
Erling Lyngtveit *Hjort*	1	6	3	5
John Christian Elden *Elden*	2	1	1	4
Erik Keiserud *Hjort*	3	NA	None	(3)
Bjørn Stordrange *Steenstrup Stordrange*	4	3	2	1
Anders Brosveet *Elden*	5	7	14	14
Ellen Holager Andenæs *Andenæs Aaløkken Veum*	6	2	8	16
Frode Sulland *Hestenes Dramer*	7	14	5	81
Cato Schiøtz *Schjødt*	8	NA	None	(3)
Berit Reiss-Andersen *Reiss-Andersen*	9	11	10	25
Else Bugge Fougner *Hjort*	10	9	16	3

lawyer. Attorney Elden had the largest number of clients, followed by Stordrange and Lyngtveit. Fourth and final column lists ranking in terms of income statement, where Stordrange made the most money.

Predictors of Lawyer Income

The white-collar crime attorney is a lawyer who is competent in general legal principles and in the substantive and procedural aspects of the law related to upper-class financial crime. Based on a sample of 310 convicted white-collar criminals and their defense lawyers, this study presents results from statistical analysis of relationships between crime characteristics and defense characteristics to predict lawyer income. Statistical correlation analysis indicates that lawyer income varies positively and significantly with the age of the criminal and the amount of money involved in crime, and it varies negatively and significantly with the number of persons involved in each criminal case. Furthermore, lawyer income varies positively and significantly with the number of white-collar crime cases handled by the lawyer, the fame factor for the lawyer, and lawyer age. When regression analysis is applied to the data, lawyer income is predicted significantly by the amount of money involved in each white-collar crime case, the fame factor for the lawyer, and the age of the lawyer.

Predictors of white-collar attorneys' income can be found among characteristics of their clients' cases as well as their own characteristics. First, characteristics of the case include age of the criminal, amount of money involved in the crime, and number of persons involved in the crime, where research hypothesis can be formulated as follows (Figure 8.1):

> *Hypothesis 1: A defense lawyer with older clients will have a higher income.*
> *Hypothesis 2: A defense lawyer handling cases involving more money will have a higher income.*
> *Hypothesis 3: A defense lawyer handling cases with more involved persons will have a higher income.*

It is assumed that older clients are able to pay their lawyers a higher fee. More money involved in the crime will make it more acceptable to pay a higher lawyer fee. If more persons are involved in the crime, then it is a rotten barrel case, rather than a rotten apple case, and an organization or a network might be blamed rather than just one person.

Characteristics of lawyers include age of the lawyer, fame of the lawyer and number of white-collar cases handled by the lawyer:

> *Hypothesis 4: An older defense lawyer will have a higher income.*
> *Hypothesis 5: A more famous lawyer will have a higher income.*
> *Hypothesis 6: A lawyer handling more white-collar cases will have a higher income.*

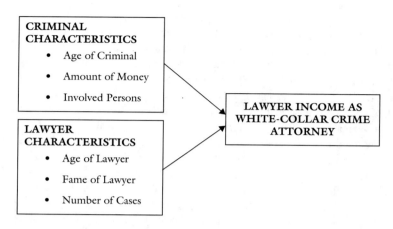

Figure 8.1 Research model to predict lawyer income

It is assumed that as lawyers get older, they will typically take on senior positions, for example as partner in a law firm. Furthermore, a more famous lawyer will be more likely to attract high-paying crime cases. More experience with crime cases will lead to high-quality knowledge work by the lawyer, who then can charge more than a lawyer with few white-collar cases.

The total sample consists of 311 convicted white-collar criminals and their lawyers, based on media reports from 2009 to 2012. Average age of criminals was 48.4 years, as listed in Table 8.5. Standard deviation for age is only 10.9, which indicates that most white-collar offenders are between 40 and 60 years old. Compared to regular street criminals, who are typically from 20 to 30 years of age, white-collar criminals are much older. The average amount of money involved in crime was 47.2 million Norwegian kroner, which is about $8 million US. Standard deviation of 158.0 million Norwegian kroner indicates a large variation in the sample.

Furthermore in Table 8.5, the number of involved persons as defined by each client and not each case was 4.1 individuals. Average age of the lawyer is about the same as average age of the client.

Some lawyers are more famous than others. How well-known a lawyer is to potential clients and in the public, might be measured in terms of media coverage. Financial newspapers represent a relevant source of fame for white-collar people. The largest Norwegian financial newspaper, *Dagens Næringsliv*, was searched for hits on their website. The most famous lawyer achieved 219 hits, followed by the

Table 8.5 Correlation analysis for white-collar criminals and their lawyers

	Average Value	Standard Deviation	Criminal Age	Crime Money	Involved Persons	Lawyer Age	Lawyer Fame	Court Cases	Lawyer Income
Criminal Age (Years)	48.4	10.9	1	.192**	−.227**	.274**	.077	.017	.195**
Crime Money (Mill NOK)	47.2	158.0		1	−.035	.135*	.139*	.070	.235**
Involved Persons	4.1	3.5			1	−.065	−.105	−.076	−.119*
Lawyer Age (Years)	51.7	10.4				1	−.003	−.093	.177**
Lawyer Fame	28.5	58.3					1	.947**	.616**
Client Cases	3.8	5.3						1	.540**
Lawyer Income	1.9	2.1							1

(** significance $p < .01$, * significance $p < .05$)

second-most famous lawyer with 112 hits on the newspaper website. The average fame factor in terms of newspaper articles was 28.5, with a large standard deviation of 58.3.

Finally, as shown in Table 8.5, each white-collar attorney was handling 3.8 white-collar client cases, with a standard deviation of 5.3 cases. Average income for lawyers was 1.9 million Norwegian kroner, which is about $300,000 US.

A number of interesting correlations are presented in Table 8.5. Among the more obvious correlations, we find a significant relationship between number of court cases and lawyer fame, which is at .947**. An interesting relationship also exists between criminal age and lawyer age, which is significant at .274**.

Our research is concerned with predictors of lawyer income, and all correlation coefficients are significant in Table 8.5:

> *Hypothesis 1: A defense lawyer with older clients will have a higher income (.195**).*
> *Hypothesis 2: A defense lawyer handling cases involving more money will have a higher income (.235**).*
> *Hypothesis 3: A defense lawyer handling cases with more involved persons will have a higher income (−119*).*
> *Hypothesis 4: An older defense lawyer will have a higher income (.177**).*

Hypothesis 5: A more famous lawyer will have a higher income (.616**).

Hypothesis 6: A lawyer handling more white-collar cases will have a higher income (.540**).

All relationships but one is positive: A defense lawyer handling cases with fewer involved persons will have a higher income. This is counter to our research hypothesis 3. An explanation might be that a lawyer is always defending only one person in court. Where there are several persons prosecuted at the same time, there will be a minimum of lawyers—equivalent to the number of prosecuted—thereby having to share both fame and potential extra fees paid by the prosecuted criminals.

To test hypotheses, there is a need to involve all six potential predictors in a single regression analysis. In total, the regression equation shows that all six independent variables are able to predict 43 percent of the variation in lawyer income, since the adjusted R^2 coefficient is .43. This coefficient is significant at .000 with an F-value of 39.4.

As listed in Table 8.6, only three out of six potential predictors are significant at $p < .05$. Crime money, lawyer age, and lawyer fame are significant predictors of lawyer income:

Hypothesis 2: A defense lawyer handling cases involving more money will have a higher income (.017).

Hypothesis 4: An older defense lawyer will have a higher income (.008).

Hypothesis 5: A more famous lawyer will have a higher income (.000).

Three out of six research hypotheses were confirmed in this research. Lawyer income increases for lawyers at higher age, who defend white-collar cases where more money was involved in the crime and who are more frequently mentioned in the business press.

A more advanced statistical technique to identify lawyer income as the dependent variable is structural equation modeling, as illustrated in Figure 8.2. In that figure, all path coefficients of PLS analysis are listed. Path coefficients are estimated for the following links in terms of hypotheses:

H1: *Client cases are positively related to lawyer fame*
H2: *Criminal age is positively related to involved persons*

EMPIRICAL STUDY OF WHITE-COLLAR LAWYERS 155

Table 8.6 Regression analysis to predict lawyer income

	Coefficients[a]				
Model	Unstandardized Coefficients		Standardized Coefficients	t	Sig.
	B	Std. Error	Beta		
(Constant)	−699238.551	646989.373		−1.081	.281
Criminal Age	15595.646	9269.673	.078	1.682	.094
Crime Money	1477.524	614.522	.108	2.404	.017
Persons	−13343.024	27056.305	−.022	−.493	.622
Lawyer Age	25897.971	9656.707	.124	2.682	.008
Lawyer Fame	28811.853	5301.823	.778	5.434	.000
Client Cases	−79468.412	57925.012	−.195	−1.372	.171

a. Dependent Variable: Lawyer Income

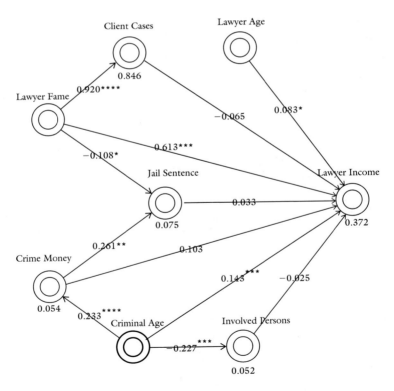

Figure 8.2 Structural equation model to predict lawyer income

H3: Criminal age is positively related to crime money
H4a: Lawyer fame is negatively related to jail sentence
H4b: Crime money are positively related to jail sentence
H5a: Lawyer income is positively related to lawyer age
H5b: Lawyer income is positively related to client cases
H5c: Lawyer income is positively related to lawyer fame
H5d: Lawyer income is positively related to crime money
H5e: Lawyer income is positively related to criminal age
H5f: Lawyer income is positively related to involved persons
H5g: Lawyer income is positively related to jail sentence (or negatively?)

A structural modeling technique, Partial Least Square (PLS) (Chin, 1998), was used to analyze the data and test the hypotheses. We used PLS Graph version 3.0 in our analysis. The results of the analysis are depicted in Figure 8.2, and estimates of the relationships are shown in Table 8.7.

In hypothesis 1, the number of client cases was found to have a positive relationship with lawyer fame (ß = 0.920, t = 55.4616, $p < 0.001$). In hypothesis 2, criminal age was found to have a positive relationship with crime money (ß = 0.233, t = 4.5609, $p < 0.001$). In hypothesis 3, criminal age was found to have a negative relationship with involved persons (ß = −0.227, t = 2.7205, $p < 0.01$).

Table 8.7 Lawyer income estimates

Dependent variable	Predictor variable	Hypothesized sign	Path coefficients	t-value	Significance level	R^2
Client cases	Lawyer fame	+	0.920	55.4616	$p < 0.001$	0.846
Crime money	Criminal age	+	0.233	4.5609	$p < 0.001$	0.054
Involved persons	Criminal age	+	−0.227	2.7205	$p < 0.01$	0.052
Jail sentence	Lawyer fame	−	−0.108	1.9321	$p < 0.1$	0.075
	Crime money	+	0.256	2.0154	$p < 0.05$	
Lawyer income	Lawyer age	+	0.083	1.7546	$p < 0.1$	0.372
	Client cases	+	−0.065	0.3639	-	
	Lawyer fame	+	0.613	3.8055	$p < 0.001$	
	Crime money	+	0.103	1.0174	-	
	Criminal age	+	0.143	2.0759	$p < 0.01$	
	Involved persons	+	−0.025	0.6674	-	
	Jail sentence	+	0.033	0.3457	-	

Hypotheses 4a and 4b examined the relationship between two different predictor variables and jail sentence. A negative relationship was found between jail sentence and lawyer fame (ß = −0.108, t = 1.9321, $p < 0.1$), and a positive relationship was found between jail sentence and crime money (ß = 0.256, t = 2.0154, $p < 0.05$)

Hypotheses 5 a–g examined the relationship between lawyer income and different predictor variables, for example. lawyer age, lawyer fame, and criminal age. In hypothesis 5a, lawyer income was found to have a positive relationship with lawyer age (ß = 0.083, t = 1.7546, $p < 0.1$). In hypothesis 5c, results indicated a positive relationship between lawyer income and lawyer fame (ß = 0.613, t = 3.8055, $p < 0.001$). In hypothesis 5e, lawyer income was found to have a positive relationship with criminal age (ß = -0.143, t = 2.0759, $p < 0.01$). No support was found for hypothesis 5b, 5d, and 5g.

Explained variance for lawyer income was 37.2 percent. There are no community standards for what is an acceptable level of explained variance (Gefen et al., 2000). In the basic research of fields like sociology, levels under 10 percent are commonly reported. Studies published in top-ranked IS/IT journals explain variance in the 20 to 30 percent range (e.g., Bock et al., 2005). In this research, the explained variances found were around these levels.

Predictors of Lawyer Fame

The white-collar crime attorney is a lawyer who is competent in general legal principles and in the substantive and procedural aspects of the law related to upper-class financial crime. Based on a sample of 310 convicted white-collar criminals and their defense lawyers, this paper presents results from statistical analysis of relationships between crime characteristics and defense characteristics to predict lawyer fame. Statistical regression analysis was applied to the sample, where amount of crime money and years in prison represent crime characteristics, while number of client cases and lawyer income represent defense characteristics. The 91 percent variation in attorney fame is explained by these four independent variables.

Predictors of white-collar attorney's fame can be found among characteristics of their clients' cases as well as their own characteristics. First, characteristics of the case include amount of money involved in the crime and the number of years in prison for the criminal, where research hypothesis can be formulated as follows (Figure 8.3):

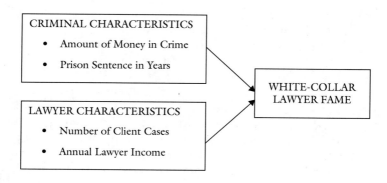

Figure 8.3 Research model to predict lawyer fame

Hypothesis 1: A defense lawyer handling a white-collar crime case involving a larger amount of money in the crime will be more famous.

Hypothesis 2: A white-collar criminal receiving a longer prison sentence will make the defense lawyer more famous.

Characteristics of lawyers include number of white-collar cases handled by lawyer as well as lawyer income:

Hypothesis 3: A defense lawyer handling more white-collar crime cases will be more famous.

Hypothesis 4: A white-collar defense lawyer making more money will be more famous.

The total sample consists of 310 convicted white-collar criminals and their lawyers, based on media reports from 2009 to 2012. Average age of criminals was 48 years when convicted in court. Compared to regular street criminals, who range from 20 to 30 years of age, white-collar criminals are much older. The average amount of money involved in crime was NOK 47.2 million, which is about $8 million US. Standard deviation of 158.0 million Norwegian kroner indicates a large variation in the sample.

Furthermore in Table 8.8, each white-collar attorney was handling 3.8 white-collar client cases, with a standard deviation of 5.3 cases. Average income for lawyers was NOK 1.9 million, which is about $300,000 US.

Some lawyers are more famous than others. How well-known a lawyer is to potential clients and to the public might be measured in terms of media coverage. Financial newspapers represent a relevant source of fame for white-collar people. The largest Norwegian financial newspaper, *Dagens Næringsliv*, was searched for hits on their website. The most famous lawyer achieved 219 hits, followed by the second-most-famous lawyer with 112 hits on the newspaper website. The average fame factor in terms of newspaper articles was 28.5, with a large standard deviation of 58.3.

Finally in Table 8.8, a number of interesting correlations are presented. Among the more obvious correlations, we find a significant relationship between crime money and prison sentence, as a more serious prison sentence is typically passed in court when the amount of Norwegian kroner involved in the crime is large.

Our research is concerned with predictors of lawyer fame, and three out of four correlation coefficients are significant in Table 8.8:

> Hypothesis 1: A defense lawyer handling a white-collar crime case involving a larger amount of money in the crime will be more famous (.139*).
>
> Hypothesis 3: A defense lawyer handling more white-collar crime cases will be more famous (.947**).

Table 8.8 Correlation analysis for white-collar criminals and their lawyers

	Average Value	Standard Deviation	Crime Money	Prison Sentence	Client Cases	Lawyer Income	Lawyer Fame
Crime Money	47.2	158.0	1	.243**	.070	.235**	.139*
Prison Sentence	2.3	1.9		1	.032	.069	.013
Client Cases	3.8	5.3			1	.540**	.947**
Lawyer Income	1.9	2.2				1	.616**
Lawyer Fame	28.5	58.3					1

(** significance $p < .01$, * significance $p < .05$)

Hypothesis 4: A white-collar defense lawyer making more money will be more famous (.616**).

To test hypotheses, there is a need to involve all four potential predictors in a single regression analysis. In total, the regression equation shows that all six independent variables are able to predict 91 percent of the variation in lawyer income, since the adjusted R^2 coefficient is .91. This coefficient is significant at .000 with an F-value of 829.061.

As listed in Table 8.9, all four potential predictors are significant at $p < .05$. Therefore, all four research hypotheses are supported in the sample of convicted white-collar criminals and their lawyers:

Hypothesis 1: A defense lawyer handling a white-collar crime case involving a larger amount of money in the crime will be more famous (.002).
Hypothesis 2: A white-collar criminal receiving a longer prison sentence in year will make the defense lawyer more famous (.029).
Hypothesis 3: A defense lawyer handling more white-collar crime cases will be more famous (.000).
Hypothesis 4: A white-collar defense lawyer making more money will be more famous (.000).

All four research hypotheses were confirmed in this research. Together, four predictor variables are able to explain as much as ninety-one percent of the variation in lawyer fame.

Table 8.9 Regression analysis for white-collar for lawyer fame

	Coefficients[a]					
Model	Unstandardized Coefficients		Standardized Coefficients		t	Sig.
	B	Std. Error	Beta			
(Constant)	−13.364	1.751			−7.632	.000
Prison	−1.146	.522	−.038		−2.196	.029
Crime Money	.021	.007	.056		3.183	.002
Client Cases	9.574	.217	.872		44.051	.000
Lawyer Income	3.617E-006	.000	.134		6.597	.000

a. Dependent Variable: Lawyer Fame

Jail Sentence and Lawyer Income

The outcome for a convicted white-collar criminal is a prison sentence in all serious court cases. The outcome for the defense lawyer is personal income. The white-collar crime attorney is a lawyer who is competent in general legal principles and in the substantive and procedural aspects of the law related to upper-class financial crime. Based on a sample of 310 convicted white-collar criminals and their defense lawyers, this analysis presents results from statistical analysis of relationships between crime characteristics and defense characteristics to predict prison sentence and lawyer income. Correlation analysis indicates that jail sentence can be predicted by the amount of money involved in crime, which in turn is influenced by age of criminals. Correlation analysis indicates further that lawyer income is predicted by a number of factors: crime money, persons involved in crime, lawyer age, lawyer fame, and number of white-collar client cases handled by the lawyer.

A total of eight variables are linked in the research model in Figure 8.4, where a distinction is made between outcome for white-collar criminal in terms of prison sentence and outcome for white-collar lawyer in terms of personal income. The main determinant of prison sentence in terms of years and months in jail is crime money, which is

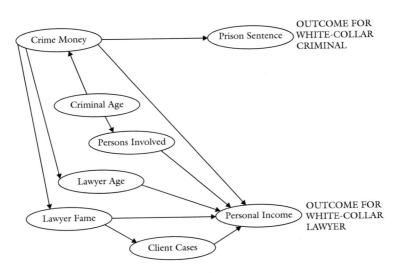

Figure 8.4 Research model to predict outcome for criminal and lawyer

the money amount that was involved in crime. Fraud cases involving large sums of money lead to more severe jail sentences. Crime money is assumed to be influenced by age of criminals, because older criminals tend to commit larger fraud. White-collar crime cases involving larger sums of money tend to attract older lawyers who are famous.

There are several determinants of personal income, which is the outcome for a white-collar lawyer in the research model. Lawyer personal income is determined by crime money as an indicator of case magnitude, number of persons involved in the crime, age of lawyer, fame of lawyer, and the number of white-collar client cases handled by the lawyer.

The total sample for this analysis consisted of 310 convicted white-collar criminals and their lawyers, based on media reports from 2009 to 2012. Average age of criminals was 48 years when convicted in court, which, as noted previously, is much older than typical street criminals. Average amount of money involved in crime was NOK 47.2 million, which is about $8 million US. Standard deviation of 158.0 million Norwegian kroner in Table 8.10 indicates a large variation in the sample.

Furthermore in Table 8.10, each white-collar attorney was handling 3.8 white-collar client cases, with a standard deviation of 5.3 cases. Average income for lawyers was NOK 1.9 million, which is about $300,000 US. Correlation coefficients are illustrated in Figure 8.5.

Some lawyers are more famous than others. How well-known a lawyer is to potential clients and the public might be measured in terms of media coverage. Financial newspapers represent a relevant source of fame for white-collar individuals. The largest Norwegian financial newspaper, *Dagens Næringsliv*, was searched for hits on their website. The most famous lawyer achieved 219 hits, followed by the second-most-famous lawyer with 112 hits on the website. The average fame factor in terms of newspaper articles was 28.5, with a large standard deviation of 58.3.

Table 8.10 shows a number of significant correlation coefficients among variables in the research model. These coefficients are included in Figure 8.5. First, crime money is indeed able to predict prison sentence length, and crime money is in turn influenced by criminal age. Other relationships are mainly concerned with direct and indirect influences on lawyer income.

A somewhat surprising result is the link between persons involved and lawyer income. White-collar crime cases involving more persons

Table 8.10 Correlation analysis for white-collar criminals and their lawyers

	Average Value	Standard Deviation	Crime Money	Prison Sentence	Client Cases	Lawyer Income	Lawyer Fame	Criminal Age	Persons Involved	Lawyer Age
Crime Money	47.2	158.0	1	.243**	.070	.235**	.139*	.192**	-.035	.135*
Prison Sentence	2.3	1.9		1	.032	.069	.013	.076	.029	.028
Client Cases	3.8	5.3			1	.540**	.947**	.017	-.076	-.093
Lawyer Income	1.9	2.2				1	.616**	.195**	-.119*	.177**
Lawyer Fame	28.5	58.3					1	.077	-.105	-.003
Criminal Age	48.3	10.9						1	-.227**	.274**
Persons Involved	4.1	3.5							1	-.065
Lawyer Age	51.7	10.3								1

** significance $p < .01$, * significance $p < .05$

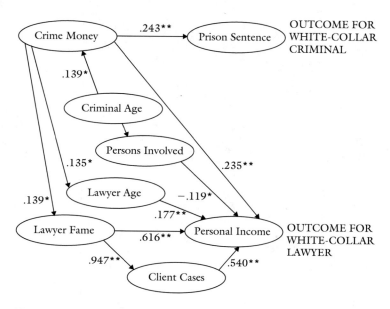

Figure 8.5 Statistical results to predict outcome for criminal and lawyer

prosecuted in court correlates negatively with lawyer income. Maybe it is because a lawyer only can defend one single person and not several of the prosecuted individuals. When more white-collar criminals are prosecuted in the same court case, case economics may lead to a lower fee for defending lawyers, as the fee is mainly determined by the number of hours each defense lawyer is able to bill to the court.

Defense Strategies and Crime

Every year, an average of one hundred white-collar criminals are sentenced to prison in Norway. Based on newspaper reports and court documents, a database of more than three hundred convicted criminals is applied in this research to answer the following research question: What links can be found from attorney defense strategies (substance defense, symbolic defense, and information control) to crime case characteristics (persons involved, money amount, and prison sentence)? A number of statistically significant relationships were identified: (i) substance defense varies positively with symbolic defense, positively with money amount in crime, and negatively with number of persons involved in crime, (ii) information control varies negatively with money amount in crime and negatively with number of persons involved in crime, and (iii) symbolic defense varies positively with substance defense, negatively with information control, and positively with money amount in crime.

The research model for this study is illustrated in Figure 8.6. While the left side links strategies for attorneys, the right side links characteristics of the criminal activity. Criminal characteristics were easy to obtain from the database, since they all represent numbers that are available: money amount in Norwegian kroner, number of involved persons, and prison sentence in terms of years and months. Attorney characteristics in terms of strategies, however, were not easily obtained. Therefore, each of them was substituted by available number for similar constructs. Substance defense was measured in terms of court levels that were passed before a final verdict occurred.

In Norway, there are three court levels: district court, court of appeal, and Supreme Court. It is assumed that substance defense was more intense over a longer period of time if the case went from district court, via court of appeal, to Supreme Court. Symbolic defense was measured in terms of fame of the lawyer, where attorney fame was associated with the number of hits in the *Norwegian Business Daily* (*Dagens Næringsliv*). It is assumed that attorneys with more appearances in the media will be more active in symbolic defense for their clients.

As illustrated in Figure 8.7, substance defense is positively linked to symbolic defense. More energy put into substance defense by the

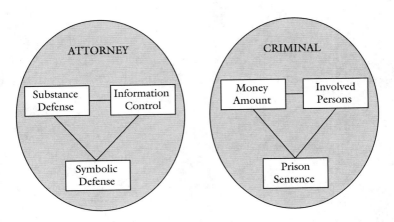

Figure 8.6 Attorney and criminal sectors with variables for each sector

attorney will be linked to more symbolic defense by the attorney. Information control is negatively linked to symbolic defense. If the attorney is active in symbolic defense, information control becomes more difficult to achieve, as symbolic defense is carried out by disseminating pieces of information to stakeholders and the press. At the criminal side in Figure 8.7, prison sentence is positively linked to money amount involved in the crime. A larger amount of money leads to a longer jail sentence.

Results in Figure 8.7 are derived from correlation coefficients in Table 8.10. Both attorney and crime variables were included in correlation analysis.

As illustrated in Figure 8.8, more severe information control is linked to crime involving a larger sum of money. Attorneys will have less possibility of information control where a large sum of money is involved in the crime, which in the next turn can lead to a more severe prison sentence. Also, information control is less successful when more people are involved in the crime.

There are more significant links between the attorney sector and the criminal sector. However, to avoid overload, these are not included in Figure 8.8, but listed in Table 8.11 instead. One such relationship is found between substance defense and money amount, where substance defense is more intense when the amount of money involved in the crime is high. Another interesting and significant relationship is between substance and persons, where substance defense is lower when there are more persons involved in crime.

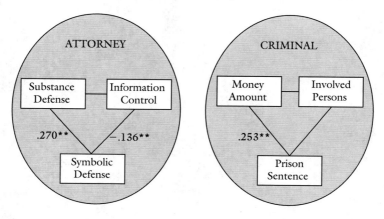

Figure 8.7 Correlations between variables within attorney and crime sectors

Table 8.11 Correlation coefficients for both attorney and crime sector variables

Correlations

		Substance	Information	Symbolic	Money	Persons	Prison
Substance	Pearson Correlation	1	-.076	.270**	.212**	-.121*	.093
	Sig. (2-tailed)		.159	.000	.000	.024	.083
	N	349	349	307	349	349	349
Information	Pearson Correlation	-.076	1	-.136*	-.135*	-.253**	-.042
	Sig. (2-tailed)	.159		.017	.012	.000	.436
	N	349	349	307	349	349	349
Symbolic	Pearson Correlation	.270**	-.136*	1	.138*	-.109	.015
	Sig. (2-tailed)	.000	.017		.015	.057	.799
	N	307	307	307	307	307	307
Money	Pearson Correlation	.212**	-.135*	.138*	1	-.023	.253**
	Sig. (2-tailed)	.000	.012	.015		.666	.000
	N	349	349	307	349	349	349
Persons	Pearson Correlation	-.121*	-.253**	-.109	-.023	1	.041
	Sig. (2-tailed)	.024	.000	.057	.666		.444
	N	349	349	307	349	349	349
Prison	Pearson Correlation	.093	-.042	.015	.253**	.041	1
	Sig. (2-tailed)	.083	.436	.799	.000	.444	
	N	349	349	307	349	349	349

**. Correlation is significant at the 0.01 level (2-tailed)
*. Correlation is significant at the 0.05 level (2-tailed).

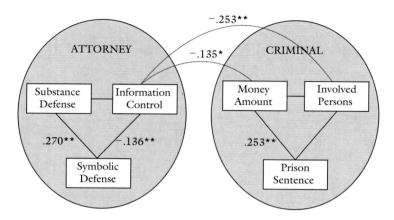

Figure 8.8 Correlations between variables of attorney and crime sectors

Furthermore, symbolic defense varies with money amount in the crime, with more symbolic defense occurring when crimes involve higher amounts of money.

Several links were identified from attorney defense strategies to crime case characteristics. These links are not necessarily of a causal nature, as this is exploratory research based on a statistical sample of convicted white-collar criminals and their defense lawyers. However, it is interesting to note that the following significant relationships exist:

- Substance defense varies positively with symbolic defense, positively with money amount in crime, and negatively with number of persons involved in crime.
- Information control varies negatively with money amount in crime and negatively with number of persons involved in crime.
- Symbolic defense varies positively with substance defense, negatively with information control, and positively with money amount in crime.

Causality will be interesting to explore in future research. For example, since prison sentence in terms of years and months in jail is influenced by money amount, it will be interesting to find out whether any of attorney defense strategies do have an impact on prison sentence.

Substance defense varies positively with symbolic defense, positively with money amount in crime, and negatively with number of persons involved in crime. Information control varies negatively with money amount in crime and negatively with number of persons involved in crime. Symbolic defense varies positively with substance defense, negatively with information control, and positively with money amount in crime. Future research will explore and exploit causal relationships that may show impacts from attorney strategies on court sentencing.

Famous White-Collar Attorneys

So far in the analyses presented in this book, the complete sample of 349 convicted white-collar criminals was applied in statistics to identify relationships in terms of correlation and regression results. In the following, analyses are limited to a subsample consisting of famous white-collar attorneys and their clients. Fame is defined in terms of coverage in the Norwegian daily business and financial newspaper *Dagens Næringsliv*. Every lawyer who is mentioned at least once in the newspaper is included in the subsample. Thereby, all attorneys never mentioned are excluded from further analyses. This exclusion procedure reduces the sample from 349 to 175 white-collar criminals.

First, we study this smaller sample of criminals to determine characteristics of crime and criminal. Later, we study this smaller sample to determine characteristics of lawyers and their clients.

Table 8.12 lists important correlation coefficients regarding the sample of criminals. Prison sentence in terms of time served in jail is positively related to age and positively related to crime amount. An older white-collar criminal involved in a crime of more money receives a longer jail sentence.

Criminal cases decided in higher Norwegian courts are characterized by older criminals, more crime money, and higher income criminals. This is indicated in Table 8.12 with significant correlation coefficients.

Correlation analysis links paired relationships, while regression analysis, to be applied next, links several independent variables to one dependent variable. A dependent variable of greatest interest in white-collar crime is the extent of jail sentence. A research model to predict the extent of jail sentence is illustrated in Figure 8.9.

Multiple regression analysis results in a regression coefficient of .308, which means that 30 percent of the variation in jail sentence can be explained by six factors: age, court level attained, amount,

Table 8.12 Correlation coefficients for white-collar criminal characteristics

	Criminal Age	Prison Sentence	Court Levels	Crime Amount	Involved Persons	Income Criminal	Business Employees
Criminal Age	1	.106*	.157**	.190**	−.202**	.119*	.158**
Prison Sentence		1	.086	.255**	.050	−.134*	−.011
Court Levels			1	.209**	−.102	.131*	.094
Crime Amount				1	−.024	−.014	.181**
Involved Persons					1	−.162**	−.075
Income Criminal						1	.141**
Business Employees							1

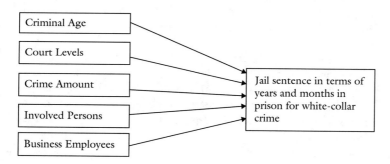

Figure 8.9 Research model for potential predictors of jail sentence

persons, income, and employees. However, the adjusted regression coefficient is only 8 percent, which is a more reliable statistic. The regression equation is significant with an F-value of 6.120 and a significance of .000.

When it comes to each of the six potential predictors, only two of them turn out to be significant. One is amount of money involved in crime, while the other is taxable income for the criminal. Therefore, a longer sentence is passed in court when the crime amount is larger and when the criminal has a higher taxable income.

Next, we study this smaller sample of 175 white-collar criminals to determine characteristics of lawyers and their clients. Table 8.13 lists important correlation coefficients regarding the sample of lawyers.

In correlation analysis, there has to be a reason for cause and effect relationships. For example, lawyer fame is significantly related to lawyer age, lawyer income, and lawyer cases. All of these relationships make sense. First, it is reasonable to assume that over time as a lawyer gets older, he or she will also become more famous. Next, a higher income lawyer will probably be more visible than a lower income lawyer. Finally, a lawyer with more white-collar defense cases will probably be more visible than a lawyer with few cases or no cases at all. If we could not make sense of such relationships, we could not assume any causality.

Correlation analysis links paired relationships, while regression analysis, to be applied next, links several independent variables to one dependent variable. A dependent variable of great interest in white-collar defense is the personal income of the lawyer: Who makes more money as an attorney? A research model to predict lawyer income is illustrated in Figure 8.10.

Table 8.13 Correlation coefficients for white-collar attorney characteristics (statistical significance is measured in terms of probability of possible mistake, where mistake is .05 at * and .01 at **)

	Criminal Age	Prison Sentence	Crime Amount	Involved Persons	Lawyer Fame	Age Lawyer	Income Lawyer	Cases Lawyer
Criminal Age	1	.102	.233**	−.227**	.073	.210**	.238**	−.003
Prison Sentence		1	.252**	.050	−.085	−.054	.017	−.028
Crime Amount			1	−.020	.087	.117	.205**	.045
Involved Persons				1	−.099	−.007	−.113	−.088
Lawyer Fame					1	−.176*	.557**	.920**
Age Lawyer						1	.036	−.306***
Income Lawyer							1	.479**
Cases Lawyer								1

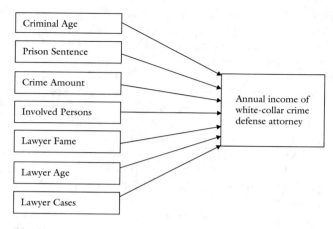

Figure 8.10 Research model for potential predictors of lawyer income

Multiple regression analysis results in a regression coefficient of .372, which means that 37 percent of the variation in annual income of white-collar crime defense attorneys can be explained by seven factors: criminal age, prison sentence, crime amount, involved persons, lawyer fame, lawyer age, and lawyer cases. Even when the regression coefficient is adjusted it remains high at .346. Again, the regression equation is significant at .000 with an F-value of 14.136.
When it comes to each of the seven potential predictors, only two of them turn out to be significant. One is the age of the criminal convicted to prison, while the other is lawyer fame in terms of newspaper hits. Therefore, white-collar defense lawyers who defend older criminals and who are more famous in the media, make more money than lawyers who defend younger criminals and who are less well-known in the press.

9

Prosecution in Court

So far, this book has discussed the role of the white-collar lawyer as a defender of white-collar criminals. The role is specified in terms of defense strategies as well as knowledge needs.

When a white-collar criminal is prosecuted in court, there are two more persons present in addition to the lawyer and the defendant. These are the prosecutor and the judge.

Prosecutors Applying the Law to White-Collar Crime

What Podgor (2007) found to be the most interesting aspect of Sutherland's work is that a scholar needed to proclaim that crime committed by a member of the "upper socioeconomic class" was in fact crime that should be prosecuted. When prosecuted in court, white-collar criminals are defended by lawyers. White-collar defense lawyers tend to be specialists in financial crime, while prosecutors tend to be generalists.

In their classic book on local prosecutors at work in combating corporate crime, Benson and Cullen (1998) discuss knowledge and discretionary decision making by legal actors as a central and unavoidable component of the law in action. Prosecutors are expressly granted authority to attain broad legislative goals. The process of rule into action cannot be accomplished unless legal actors interpret and make choices. In this perspective, prosecutors are powerful actors in criminal justice.

However, white-collar crime can also be perceived as a prosecutorial problem. Benson and Cullen (1998: 25) argue that most illegal corporate conduct does not result in criminal prosecution:

> Scholars differ over why this is so. One school of thought stresses the political and economic power of corporations; the other emphasizes

the practical difficulties of applying the criminal law to corporate offenders. These views represent recurrent themes in research on corporate crime but are not necessarily mutually exclusive. Undoubtedly, both have merit (25).

To better understand how prosecutors view the traditional goals of criminal law, Benson and Cullen (1998) asked surveyed prosecutors to rank their most important prosecutorial goals in three different situations: individuals who commit traditional street crime; individual businesspeople who commit corporate crime; and corporations or other business entities that commit corporate crime. A question of particular importance was whether prosecutors, like judges, pursue different goals when confronted with street criminals as opposed to individual corporate executives or corporate entities.

Benson and Cullen (1998) found that prosecutors pursue different punishment objectives depending on the type of offense and the type of offender. In cases involving individuals who commit traditional street crime, over 60 percent of prosecutors chose either special deterrence or incapacitation as their most important objective. In contrast, for individual businesspeople who commit corporate crime, general deterrence was the modal category, with 39 percent ranking it as most important objective of prosecution. Thus, prosecutors appear to pursue broader objectives in handling corporate crime than they do when dealing with street criminals. Their focus is less on the impact of punishment on the offender and more on the impact of punishment on the community as a whole.

Judges Sentencing White-Collar Criminals

While this book has described a number of sentences in terms of imprisonment of white-collar criminals in Norway, there is another interesting aspect of sentencing—the time spent making judicial decisions in court. Most discussions of judicial efficiency either point out the need for court reform, resulting from perceived inefficiency, or analyze the logical implications of various types of reform without empirically testing these implications (Christensen and Szmer, 2012).

White-collar crime cases presented in this book from Norwegian courts did indeed take a long time. Typically, police spend a year investigating the case. Then, the case is opened for court hearings after another year. The court proceedings normally last for a few weeks in district courts. Then, the verdict is denied and the case is presented to a court of appeals after another year. The verdict from a court of appeals may then be presented several years after police started their investigation. Often, we are here talking about three or four years from initial suspicion to final jail sentence. If the Supreme Court gets involved, it takes even more time.

Therefore, Christensen and Szmer's 2012 study of the efficiency of US courts of appeals is of interest. They found that institutional mechanisms have the greatest impact on efficiency. Vacancies, size (number of judges and area of community covered), and oral arguments were statistically significant. Oral arguments had the largest effect on efficiency. While having certain potential benefits, oral arguments add more than a month to the disposition time.

Christensen and Szmer defined efficiency in terms of disposition time, which might be defined in this way (http://www.utcourts.gov/courtools/reports.asp?measure=disposition&court=dist&detail=all):

> Time to disposition is the average number of days in which cases are disposed or resolved during a given time period. The number of days is calculated by counting the number of days from case filing to entry of judgment on charges or the case.

The district courts in Norway are organized as 107 separate units, each with a geographical basis that includes one or several municipalities. They are the lowest level in a three-tier judicial system in a country with 5 million inhabitants. Kittelsen and Førsund (1992) studied the efficiency of Norwegian district courts. Results show estimates of overstaffing due to technical inefficiency. Comparisons were made between the specialized city courts and the generalized rural courts.

Just like the prosecutor and the defense attorney, the judge is a knowledge worker. The judge is supposed to be completely independent and impartial. No one is to instruct the judge about contents or conclusions in court sentences. There are no quantitative or qualitative success criteria for judges. In Norway, they all have the same salary at the same court level. Some work a lot, some work less. Work is completely individualized, as is quite common in knowledge organizations, where work output is nothing but knowledge.

If the Supreme Court lifts or changes a decision from courts of appeal, everyone talks about it, but it has no consequence or implies no feedback to the judge(s) in the appeal court. Some judges may perceive a change in their own verdict as a provocation, but they never voice it.

The only difference between judges can be found in their relative prestige among colleagues. Some judges receive a lot of attention from colleagues, others do not. In difficult cases, some colleagues are consulted. They are typically loaded with knowledge and at the same time open and helpful. They get paid in terms of attention and respect, not in terms of money.

Casanovas et al. (2005) carried out a survey among Spanish judges. One of the questions in the questionnaire was with whom judges discuss their cases. In first place came public prosecutors. [CE4] Of those who responded, 32 percent of judges said they discuss each case with public prosecutors, 23 percent said they discuss each case with fellow judges, 15 percent said they discussed with other colleagues, and 11 percent discuss with a supervisor or tutor.

The ambition of a judge is to get both parties to understand and accept his or her decision as a relevant and correct expression of both facts and law, so that the verdict is not appealed. If the decision is appealed, it is perceived as positive if a higher court confirms the verdict. This is especially true when a verdict is appealed from a court of appeal to the Supreme Court.

The judge has a master's degree in law. Since all law schools in Norway are part of public universities, where there is no tuition to be paid, a clear ranking of law schools does not exist, although informally Oslo is ranked before Bergen and Tromsø. Grades achieved are more important. Often, judge, prosecutor, and lawyer know about one another's grades back at university. A distinction in the legal society is made between those who averaged A or B and those who did not. In the old grading system in Norwegian law schools, there were only those with "laud" (about 10 percent), and those with "haud" (all the others).

This situation is very different in the United States. As discussed by Christensen and Szmer (2012), elite law schools include Harvard, Yale, Chicago, Stanford, Columbia, Michigan, Berkeley, Pennsylvania, New York University, Duke, Virginia, Texas, Cornell, Northwestern, and University of California Los Angeles (UCLA).

Knowledge Characteristics of Legal Courts

While there are differences between court systems throughout the world, legal courts in democratic societies have some common characteristics. A court is an institution for finding solutions and making decisions in conflicts. District court is the basic level in the judiciary system in Norway for both criminal and civil law. Court of appeal is the second level in the system, where district court decisions are appealed. There are six courts of appeal in Norway, which carry names from the time of Vikings: Borgarting, Hålogaland, Frostating, Eidsivating, Agder, and Gulating. Most of the courts carry the term "ting" in their names, which meant "annual meeting place for Vikings." In Norway, there are currently 5 million inhabitants. The Supreme Court is located in Oslo, the capital of Norway.

As suggested earlier in this book, there is a rivalry of knowledge going on in courts. Knowledge competition between prosecution and defense is illustrated again in Figure 9.1, and a new dimension is added: the knowledge level of the judge. The more familiar the judge is with the topic in a specific white-collar crime case, both in legal and business knowledge categories, the less room there is for knowledge competition between prosecution and defense. The area market "competition" is smaller when there is an experienced judge, while it is greater when there is an inexperienced judge.

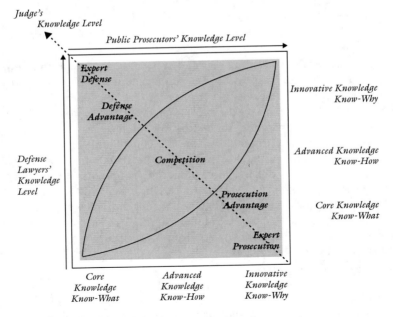

Figure 9.1 Knowledge rivalry controlled by judge expertise

Relative grades from law school may also influence knowledge rivalry in court. Prosecutor, lawyer, and judge will know whether the others got *laud* or *haud* in law school, and As or Bs or worse. Even if the judge is supposed to be the boss in court, a famous white-collar defense lawyer with laud or an A will sometimes be the real boss in court, especially if both prosecutor and judge were not as successful in law school and they all know about it.

Relative grades from law school change at different court levels. Supreme Court judges do normally have excellent grades; otherwise they would not have been appointed by the government. While the defense lawyer may take the case all the way, his or her relative knowledge position changes as the case moves from district court via court of appeal to Supreme Court. The same can be said about the prosecutor.

To defend and prosecute in the Supreme Court, a lawyer and prosecutor must first be admitted. Admittance is dependent on a few trial cases. So the worst defense lawyers are never admitted to the Supreme Court. Hence, there is a tendency to only have expert judges, lawyers, and prosecutors present in the Supreme Court.

In our knowledge perspective, a decision in district court can be influenced by the relative position of judge, lawyer, and prosecutor. If the judge is a generalist with limited experience and bad grades in law school, and the prosecutor is in the same range as well, the white-collar defense lawyer may have a wide range of opportunities to make the court dismiss the case. Both in terms of facts, law, and previous cases, the defense lawyer may convince the others about an interpretation that makes the client not guilty.

In terms of income, prosecutors are the losers in Norwegian courts. In 2013, a prosecutor made 140,000 US dollars. A district court judge made 160,000 US dollars, a judge at court of appeals made 200,000 US dollars, and a judge at the Supreme Court made 250,000 US dollars. As calculated earlier, a white-collar defense attorney made on average 320,000 US dollars in 2009, which can be stipulated to 350,000 US dollars in 2013. As a consequence, some clever prosecutors change from prosecution to defense law before the age of 40.

Prison Sentence by Knowledge Rivalry

In terms of sentencing white-collar criminals in court, Maddan et al. (2012) found that ethnicity and class have an impact on severity of jail sentence. A large body of empirical studies has focused on personality variables. In general, white-collar criminals have been found to be different from other criminals. A larger percentage is male, older, graduates of high school and college, and they are less likely to be unemployed (Poortinga et al., 2006; Walters and Geyer, 2004; Wheeler et al., 1988). It is less likely that these criminals have an arrest history or meet diagnostic criteria for substance abuse (Benson and Moore, 1992; Ragatz et al., 2012).

Compared to the focus on offender characteristics, research on the disparity of sentencing is sparse. However, according to Maddan et al. (2012), the research has grown during the last two decades. Compared to street or common offenders, the most frequent notion is that white-collar criminals are treated more leniently. Such characteristics, perhaps especially socioeconomic status, are strongly associated with offense type (Maddan et al.). Accordingly, white-collar crime is interesting to study in the light of institutionalized system bias. Madden et al. applied data on the relationship between sentencing practice and type of offense (white-collar versus street-level offenders) from the United States Sentencing Commission for the year 1993 and found a significant difference in judicial imprisonment decisions between white collar and other criminals. There was also a significant correspondence between offense seriousness and criminal history of the convicts and the number of months sentenced. This is in line with Hagan et al (1982), who found that people with higher incomes more often received more lenient sentences. Similarly, Wheeler et al. (1982) showed that there was a significant relationship between severity of sentence and socioeconomic status. It may be, however, that fines for white-collar criminals mediate sentences, in other words, the larger the fines the shorter the sentences received (Shanzenbach and Yaeger, 2006).

Several studies have also investigated perceived seriousness of white-collar crime among lay people and among criminal justice system personnel. Wheeler et al. (1988) found that lay people did not view white-collar crime as being serious in comparison to crimes committed against other persons or the public. A study carried out by Cullen et al. (1982) also showed that white-collar crime was rated to be less serious. However, lay people's perception of the seriousness of white-collar crime was found to have increased over time. In a study of perceptions carried out among a student sample, white-collar crime was also found to be rated less serious than violent crime but more serious than property crime (Rosenmerkel, 2001).

In another study carried out among a national sample by Piquero et al. (2008), the majority of the respondents perceived white-collar crime to be either equal to or more serious than street crime. Almost two thirds of the sample believed that the resources to mitigate white-collar crime should be at least or more than that which is spent on street crime. These results question the assertion that lay people perceive street crime to be more serious compared to white-collar crime. Studies comparing perception of seriousness of white collar crime among lay people and criminal justice system personnel have shown that the perception is similar across the groups (Pontell et al., 1983; McCleary et al., 1981).

It is in this diffuse and unclear status of white-collar crime in society that knowledge rivalry between defense lawyer, state prosecutor, and court judge takes place. Variations in perceived seriousness of white-collar crime among lay people as well as among politicians and criminal justice system personnel represent a large space for knowledge competition among all actors in court.

Conclusion

White-collar crime defense is significantly different from other kinds of crime defense. A defense lawyer in a white-collar case spends much more time on the case itself and on each single case, both in terms of total workload and in terms of total calendar time. Therefore, a white-collar lawyer will work on far fewer cases in parallel as compared to a lawyer who specializes in street crime. White-collar crime lawyers apply three distinct strategies in their defense of white-collar criminals.

Substance defense strategy is applied early on to prevent a prosecution decision. The defense lawyer will try to convince the police and prosecution that the client has done nothing that justifies court proceedings and a potential jail sentence. The strategic issue for the attorney is how to succeed in stopping the state prosecutor from advancing the investigation and case from suspicion to prosecution in court. While very different from other crime cases, an attorney's active defense work in a white-collar crime case often starts in the initial phases of a police investigation, when there is only rumor of wrongdoing that may or may not be a relevant violation of criminal law.

Information control strategy is also applied early on by the defense lawyer to prevent the police from gaining access to information that can harm the client's case. Instead of being at the receiving end of documents from the police and prosecution, the attorney is in a position where the flow of information can be monitored. The flow of harmful facts, insights, and knowledge of causes and effects that might become legal evidence with the police is restricted and stopped by the lawyer. While the police have many information sources, an attorney may attempt to influence several of them.

Information benefits can be reduced in terms of quality and security by the defense lawyer.

Symbolic defense strategy is applied to divert attention from the crime and to add complexity to court proceedings. Symbolic defense is concerned with activities that represent and stand for defense, but in themselves are no defense. Symbolic defense is an alternative and a supplement to substance defense. Complaining about delays in police investigations or portraying the client as a victim are typical examples of symbolic defense. The purpose of symbolic defense is to communicate meaning and opinions by means of symbols and symbolic actions.

As illustrated in this book, both white-collar criminals as well as their attorneys demonstrate entrepreneurial capabilities. While the white-collar criminal applies entrepreneurial skills to commit and conceal financial crime, the white-collar attorney applies entrepreneurial skills in damage limitation to author a plausible defense based on their legal experience and knowledge with the intention of extracting their client from their predicament.

Literature

Alalehto, T. and Larsson, D. (2009). "The Roots of Modern White-Collar Crime: Does the Modern Form of White-Collar Crime Have Its Foundation in the Transition from a Society Dominated by Agriculture to One Dominated by Industry." *Critical Criminology*, 17, 183–193.

Albrecht, C. C., Albrecht, W. S., and Dunn, J. G. (2001). "Can Auditors Detect Fraud: A Review of the Research Evidence." *Journal of Forensic Accounting*, II:1–12.

Anderson, J. M. and Heaton, P. (2012). How Much Difference Does the Lawyer Make? The Effect of Defense Counsel on Murder Case Outcomes." *The Yale Law Journal*, 122:154, 153–217.

Ashforth, B. E., Gioia, D. A., Robinson, S. L., and Trevino, L. K. (2008). Re-Reviewing Organizational Corruption. *The Academy of Management Review*, 33 (3), 670–684.

Atkins, R. D., editor (1995). *The Alleged Transnational Criminal*. The Hague, Netherlands: Martinus Nijhoff Publishers.

Attanasio, M. A. (2008). "Handling Criminal Investigations." *Financial Executive*, December, 56–58.

Babiak, P. (2007). "From Darkness into the Light: Psychopathy in Industrial Organizational Psychology." in: H. Herve and J. C. Yuillwe (editors). *The Psychopath: Theory, Research, and Practice*. Mahwah, NJ: Lawrence Erlbaum Associates. 411–428.

Babiak, P., Neumann, C. S., and Hare, R. D. (2010). Corporate Psychopathy: Talking the Walk." *Behavioral Sciences and the Law*, 28, 174–193.

Baitar, R., Buysse, A., Brondeel, R., Mol, J., and Rober, P. (2012). "Toward High-Quality Divorce Agreements: The Influence of Facilitative Professionals." *Negotiation Journal*, October, 452–473.

Banaji, M. R., Bazerman, M. H., and Chugh, D. (2003). "How (Un)Ethical Are You?" *Harvard Business Review*, December, 56–64.

Barak, G. (2007). Doing Newsmaking Criminology from within the Academy, *Theoretical Criminology*, 11 (2), 191–207.

Beare, M. E. (2007). "The Devil Made Me Do It: Business Partners in Crime." *Journal of Financial Crime*, 14 (1), 34–48.

Beasley, M. S. (2003). "SAS No. 99: A New Look at Auditor Detection of Fraud." *Journal of Forensic Accounting* IV:1–20.

Becker, W. M., Herman, M. F., Samuelson, P. A., and Webb, A. P. (2001). "Lawyers Get Down to Business." *The McKinsey Quarterly*, 2, 45–55.

Benson, M. L. and Moore, E. (1992). "Are White Collar and Common Offenders the Same?" An Empirical Examination and Theoretical Critique of a Recently Proposed General Theory of Crime." *Journal of Research in Crime and Delinquency*, 29, 251–272.

Benson, M. L. and Cullen, F. T. (1998). *Combating Corporate Crime: Local Prosecutors at Work*. Boston: Northeastern University Press.

Benson, M. L. and Simpson, S. S. (2009). *White-Collar Crime: An Opportunity Perspective, Criminology and Justice Series*. NY, New York: Routledge.

Blickle, G., Schlegel, A., Fassbender, P., and Klein, U. (2006). "Some Personality Correlates of Business White-Collar Crime." *Applied Psychology: An International Review*, 55 (2), 220–233.

Bock, G.-W., Zmud, R. W., and Kim, Y.-G. (2005). "Behavioral Intention Formation in Knowledge-Sharing: Examining the Roles of Extrinsic Motivators, Social-Psychological Forces, and Organizational Climate." *MIS Quarterly*, 29(1), 87–111.

Brightman, H. J. (2009). *Today's White-Collar Crime: Legal, Investigative, and Theoretical Perspectives*. NY, New York: Routledge, Taylor & Francis Group.

Brisman, A. (2010). "'Creative Crime' and the Phytological Analogy." *Crime Media Culture*, 6 (2), 205–225.

Bryans, H. S. (2009). "Business Successors and the Transpositional Attorney-Client Relationship." *The Business Lawyer*, 64, 1039–1086.

Bucy, P. H., Formby, E. P., Raspanti, M. S., and Rooney, K. E. (2008). "Why Do They Do It? The Motives, Mores, and Character of White-Collar Criminals." *St. John's Law Review*, 82 (2), 401–571.

Casanovas, P., Poblet, M., Casellas, N., Contreras, J., Benjamins, R., and Blazquez, M. (2005). "Supporting Newly-Appointed Judges: A Legal Knowledge Management Case Study." *Journal of Knowledge Management*, 9 (5), 7–27.

Chaffey, D. and White, G. (2011). *Business Information Management*, Second Edition, London, UK: Prentice Hall.

Cheng, H. and Ma, L. (2009). "White-Collar Crime and the Criminal Justice System—Government Response to Bank Fraud and Corruption in China." *Journal of Financial Crime*, 16 (2), 166–179.

Chin, W. W. (1998). "Issues and Opinion on Structural Equation Modeling." *MIS Quarterly*, 22(1), vii–xvi.

Christensen, C. M. and Raynor, M. E. (2003). "Why Hard-Nosed Executives Should Care About Management Theory." *Harvard Business Review*, September, 66–74.

Christensen, R. K. and Szmer, J. (2012). "Examining the Efficiency of the U.S. Courts of Appeals: Pathologies and Prescriptions." *International Review of Law and Economics*, 32, 30–37.

Collins, J. M. and Schmidt, F. L. (1993). "Personality, Integrity, and White Collar Crime: A Construct Validity Study." *Personnel Psychology*, 46 (2), 295–311.

Collins, J. D., Uhlenbruck, K., and Rodriguez, P. (2009). "Why Firms Engage in Corruption: A Top Management Perspective." *Journal of Business Ethics*, 87, 89–108.

Colquitt, J. A. and Zapata-Phelan, C. P. (2007). "Trends in Theory Building and Theory Testing: A Five-Decade Study of the Academy of Management Journal." *Academy of Management Journal*, 50 (6), 1281–1303.

Croall, H. (2007). *Victims, Crime, and Society*. Los Angeles: Sage.

Cullen, F. T., Link, B. G., and Polanzi, C. W. (1982). "The Seriousness of Crime Revisited: Have Attitudes Towards White Collar Crime Changed?" *Criminology*, 20, 83–102.

Dhami, M. K. (2007). "White-Collar Prisoners' Perceptions of Audience Reaction." *Deviant Behavior*, 28, 57–77.

Dibbern, J., Winkler, J., and Heinzl, A. (2008). "Explaining Variations in Client Extra Costs between Software Projects Offshored to India." *MIS Quarterly*, 32 (3), 333–366.

Dion, M. (2008). "Ethical Leadership and Crime Prevention in the Organizational Setting." *Journal of Financial Crime*, 15 (3), 308–319.

Dion, M. (2009). "Corporate Crime and the Dysfunction of Value Networks." *Journal of Financial Crime*, 16 (4), 436–445.

Dion, M. (2010). "Corruption and Ethical Relativism: What Is at Stake?" *Journal of Financial Crime*, 17 (2), 240–250.

Drage, K. and Olstad, T. (2008). Ekstern revisor og økonomisk kriminalitet - En analyse av revisors ansvar og brukernes forventninger Regnskap og revisjon. BI Norwegian School of Management, Oslo.

Du Plessis, T. (2008). Competitive Legal Professionals' Use of Technology in Legal Practice and Legal Research, *PER Electronic Law Journal*, (3).

Eberly, M. B., Holley, E. C., Johnson, M. D., and Mitchell, T. R. (2011). "Beyond Internal and External: A Dyadic Theory of Relational Attributions." *Academy of Management Review*, 36 (4), 731–753.

Edelhertz, H. (1983). "White-Collar and Professional Crime." *American Behavioral Scientist*, 27 (1), 109–128.

Eicher, S. (2009). "Government for Hire," in Eicher, S. editor, *Corruption in International Business—The Challenge of Cultural and Legal Diversity*. Corporate Social Responsibility Series, Gower Applied Business Research. Farnham, England: Ashgate Publishing Limited.

Eisenhardt, K. M. (1985). "Control: Organizational and Economic Approaches. *Management Science,* 31(2), 134–149.

Farrell, B. R. and Healy, P. (2000). "White Collar Crime: A Profile of the Perpetrator and an Evaluation of the Responsibilities for its Prevention and Detection." *Journal of Forensic Accounting* I:17–34.

Füss, R. and Hecker, A. (2008). "Profiling White-Collar Crime: Evidence from German-Speaking Countries." *Corporate Ownership & Control*, 5 (4), 149–161.

Galanter, M. and Palay, T. (1991). *Tournament of Lawyers. The Transformation of the Big Law Firm*. Chicago: The University of Chicago Press.

Garoupa, N. (2007). "Optimal Law Enforcement and Criminal Organization." *Journal of Economic Behavior & Organization*, 63, 461–474.

Gefen, D., Straub, D. W., and Boudreau, M.-C. (2000). "Structural Equation Modeling and Regression: Guidelines for Research Practice." *Communications of the Association for Information Systems*, 4(7), 1–79.

Gillers, S. (2012). "A Profession, If You Can Keep It: How Information Technology and Fading Borders are Reshaping the Law Marketplace and What We Should Do About It." *Hastings Law Journal*, 63, 953–1022.

Goldstraw-White, J. (2012). *White-Collar Crime: Accounts of Offending Behaviour*. London: Palgrave Macmillan.

Gottfredson, M. R. and Hirschi, T. (1990). *A General Theory of Crime*. Stanford, CA: Stanford University Press.

Gottschalk, P. and Smith, R. (2011). "Criminal Entrepreneurship, White-Collar Criminality, and Neutralization Theory." *The Journal of Enterprising Peoples, Communities, and Places in the Global Economy*, 5 (4), 300–308.

Grini, S. (2013a). "Koch vant advokatkrig (Koch won lawyer war)." *Finansavisen* daily newspaper, May 29, 6.

Gross, E. (1978). "Organizational Crime: A Theoretical Perspective." *Studies in Symbolic Interaction*, 1, 55–85.

Gupta, U., editor (2005). *The Entrepreneurial Lawyer: How Testa, Hurwitz, Thibeault Shaped a High-Tech Culture*. Canada: Bayeux Arts Inc.

Haakaas, E. (2009). "Acta-saken kan smuldre bort (Acta case can mold away)." *Afteposten* daily newspaper, November 27, Business section, 2.

Haantz, S. (2002). *Women and White Collar Crime*. National White Collar Crime Center, www.nw3c.org.

Hagan, J., Nagel, I. H., and Albonetti, C. A. (1982). "The Social Organization of White Collar Sanctions: A Study of Prosecutions and Punishment in the Federal Courts," in: P. Wickmann and T. Dailey (editors). *White Collar and Economic Crime: Multidisciplinary and Cross-National Perspectives*, Lanham, MD: Lexington Books, Rowan & Littlefield. 259–275.

Hansen, L. L. (2009). "Corporate Financial Crime: Social Diagnosis and Treatment." *Journal of Financial Crime*, 16 (1), 28–40.

Hanssen, I. D. (2007). "Røkke vedtar dommen (Røkke agrees to sentence)." *Aftenposten*, www.aftenposten.no, published April 21, 2011.

Harfield, C. (2008). Paradigms, Pathologies, and Practicalities—Policing Organized Crime in England and Wales, *Policing*, 2 (1), 63–73.

Harvard Law Review (2009). "Go Directly to Jail: White Collar Sentencing After the Sarbanes-Oxley Act." 122, 1728–1749.

Hobbs, D. (1989). *Doing the Business, Entrepreneurship, the Working Class, and Detectives in the East End of London*. Oxford: Oxford University Press.

Holtfreter, K., Beaver, K. M., Reisig, M. D., and Pratt, T. C. (2010). "Low Self-Control and Fraud Offending." *Journal of Financial Crime*, 17 (3), 295–307.

Huffman, M. L., Cohen, P. N., and Pearlman, J. (2010). "Engendering Change: Organizational Dynamics and Workplace Gender Desegregation." *Administrative Science Quarterly*, 55, 255–277.

Iossa, E. and Jullien, B. (2012). "The Market for Lawyers and Quality Layers in Legal Services." *RAND Journal of Economics*, 43 (4), 677–704.

Jensen, M. C. and Meckling, W. H. (1976). "Theory of the Firm: Managerial Behavior, Agency Costs and Ownership Structures." *Journal of Financial Economics*, 3(4), 305–360.

Johnson, G. G. and Rudesill, C. L. (2001). "An Investigation into Fraud Prevention and Detection of Small Businesses in the United States: Responsibilities of Auditors, Managers, and Business Owners." *Accounting Forum* 25 (1):56.

Jonassen, A. M. (2011b). "Har tatt bevillingen fra 100 advokater." *Aftenposten*, February 20, 4–5.

Jones, M. (2009). "Governance, Integrity, and the Police Organization." *Policing: An International Journal of Police Strategies & Management*, 32 (2), 338–350.

Judge, T. A., Piccolo, R. F., and Kosalka, T. (2009). "The Bright and Dark Sides of Leader Traits: A Review and Theoretical Extension of the Leader Trait Paradigm." *The Leadership Quarterly*, 20, 855–875.

Kempa, M. (2010). "Combating White-Collar Crime in Canada: Serving Victim Needs and Market Integrity." *Journal of Financial Crime*, 17 (2), 251–264.

Kirkebøen, S. E. (2011). "Politiet vil lese advokatpost (Police want to read lawyer mail)." *Aftenposten*, January 29, 7.

Kiser, G. C. (1986). "Book Review of *Defending White-Collar Crime*," *Social Science Quarterly*, 655–656.

Kittelsen, S. A. C. and Førsund, F. R. (1992). "Efficiency Analysis of Norwegian District Courts." *The Journal of Productivity Analysis*, 3, 277–306.

Klesty, V. and Reddall, B. (2011). "Norway Indicts Transocean over Alleged Tax Fraud." *Thompson Reuters News & Insights*, downloaded January 2, 2012, http://newsandinsight.thomsonreuters.com/Legal/News/2011/06_-_June/Norway_indicts_Transocean_over_alleged_tax_fraud/

Kopon, A. and Sungaila, M. C. (2012). "The Perils of Oversharing: Can the Attorney-Client Privilege be Broadly Waived by Partially Disclosing Attorney Communications During Negotiations?" *Defense Counsel Journal*, July, 265–277.

KPMG (2009). *KPMG Malaysia fraud survey report 2009*. KPMG, Kuala Lumpur, Malaysia.
KPMG (2011). "Who Is the Typical Fraudster?" KPMG, www.kpmg.com. http://www.kpmg.com/BY/ru/IssuesAndInsights/ArticlesPublications/Press%20Releases/Documents/Who%20is%20the%20typical%20fraudster.pdf
Langbach, T. (1996). *Forsvareren (The Defense Lawyer)*, Juridisk Forlag, Oslo.
Lange, D. (2008). "A Multidimensional Conceptualization of Organizational Corruption Control." *The Academy of Management Review*, 33 (3), 710–729.
Li, S. and Ouyang, M. (2007). "A Dynamic Model to Explain the Bribery Behavior of Firms." *International Journal of Management*, 24 (3), 605–618.
Listwan, S. J., Piquero, N. L., and Voorhis, P. (2010). "Recidivism among a White-Collar Sample: Does Personality Matter?" *Australian & New Zealand Journal of Criminology*, 43, 156–174.
Lombardo, R. M. (2002). "Black Hand: Terror by Letter in Chicago." *Journal of Contemporary Criminal Justice*, 18 (4), 394–409.
Lyman, M. D. and Potter, G. W. (2007). *Organized crime*, 4th edition. Upper Saddle River, New Jersey: Pearson Prentice Hall.
Maddan, S., Hartley, R. D., Walker, J. T., and Miller, J. M. (2012). "Sympathy for the Devil: An Exploration of Federal Judicial Discretion in Processing of White Collar Offenders." *American Journal of Criminal Justice*, 37, 4–18.
Mann, K. (1985). *Defending White-Collar Crime: A Game Without Rules*. New Haven, CT: Yale University Press.
McCleary, R., O'Neil, M. J., Epperlein, T., Jones, C. and Gray, R. H. (1981). "Effects of Legal Education and Work Experience on Perceptions of Crime Seriousness." *Social Problems*, 28, 276–289.
McKay, R., Stevens, C., and Fratzi, J. (2010). "A 12-Step Process of White-Collar Crime." *International Journal of Business Governance and Ethics*, 5 (1), 14–25.
Meneses, R. A. and Akers, R. L. (2011). "A Comparison of Four General Theories of Crime and Deviance: Marijuana Use Among American and Bolivian University Students," *International Criminal Justice Review*, 21 (4), 333–352.
Miller, N. P., Dunn, M. J., and Crane, J. D. (2012). *Entrepreneurial Practice: Enterprise Skills for Lawyers Serving Emerging Client Populations*. Netherlands: Vandeplas Publishing.
Miri-Lavassani, K., Kumar, V., Movahedi, B., and Kumar, U. (2009). "Developing an Identity Measurement Model: A Factor Analysis Approach, *Journal of Financial Crime*, 16 (4), 364–386.
Misangyi, V. F., Weaver, G. R., and Elms, H. (2008). "Ending Corruption: The Interplay Among Institutional Logics, Resources, and Institutional Entrepreneurs," *The Academy of Management Review*, 33 (3), 750–798.

Morton, J. (2013). *Gangland: The Lawyers*, London: Virgin Books.

Mountain, D. (2001). "Could New Technologies Cause Great Law Firms to Fall?" *Journal of Information, Law & Technology*, elj.warwick.ac.uk. http://www2.warwick.ac.uk/fac/soc/law/elj/jilt/2001_1/mountain/

Moyes, G. D. and Baker, C. R. (2003). "Auditors' Beliefs about the Fraud Detection Effectiveness of Standard Audit Procedures." *Journal of Forensic Accounting* IV:199–216.

News from Norway (2011). Convicted executive faces two years in prison, *Norway International Network*, www.newsinenglish.no, published October 5, 2011.

News from Norway (2012). Rig evasion case underway, *Views and News from Norway*, downloaded January 2, 2012, http://www.newsinenglish.no/2012/12/09/rig-tax-evasion-case-underway/

Nottage, L. (1998). "Cyberspace and the Future of Law, Legal Education, and Practice in Japan." *Journal of Current Legal Issues*, webjcli.ncl.ac.uk. http://webjcli.ncl.ac.uk/1998/issue5/nottage5.html

Oh, J. J. (2004). "How (Un)ethical Are You? Letters to the Editor." *Harvard Business Review*, March, 122.

Olsen, A. B. (2007). *Økonomisk kriminalitet: avdekking, granskning og forebygging (Economic crime: detection, investigation and prevention)*. Oslo: Universitetsforlaget.

Osiel, M. J. (1990). "Lawyers as Monopolists, Aristocrats, and Entrepreneurs." *Harvard Law Review*, 103 (8), 2009–2066.

Østerbø, K. (2013). "Fengselet ble ikke den leirskolen jeg hadde trodd" (Prison Was Not Like the Camp I Thought It Would Be), *Aftenposten*, March 16, p. 20.

Parsons, M. (2004). *Effective Knowledge Management for Law Firms*. Oxford: Oxford University Press.

Pfarrer, M. D., DeCelles, K. A., Smith, K. G., and Taylor, M. S. (2008). "After the Fall: Reintegrating the Corrupt Organization." *The Academy of Management Review*, 33 (3), 730–749.

Phillips, D. J. (2005). "Organizational Genealogies and the Persistence of Gender Inequality: The Case of Silicon Valley Law Firms." *Administrative Science Quarterly*, 50, 440–472.

Pickett, K. H. S. and Pickett, J. M. (2002). *Financial Crime Investigation and Control*. New York: John Wiley & Sons.

Pinto, J., Leana, C. R. and Pil, F. K. (2008). "Corrupt Organizations or Organizations of Corrupt Individuals? Two Types of Organization-Level Corruption." *The Academy of Management Review*, 33 (3), 685–709.

Piquero, N. L. (2012). "The Only Thing We Have to Fear Is Fear Itself: Investigation the Relationship between Fear of Falling and White-Collar Crime." *Crime and Delinquency*, 58 (3), 362–379.

Piquero, N. L., Carmichael, S. and Piquero, A. R. (2008). "Assessing the Perceived Seriousness of White Collar And Street Crimes." *Crime and Delinquency*, 54 (2), 291–312.

Podgor, E. S. (2007). "The Challenge of White Collar Sentencing." *Journal of Criminal Law and Criminology*, Spring, 97 (3), 1–10.

Pontell, H. N. (2005). "Control Fraud, Gambling Resurrection, and Moral Hazard: Accounting for White-Collar Crime in the Savings and Loan Crisis." *The Journal of Socio-Economics*, 34, 75–770.

Pontell, H. N., Granite, D., Keenan, C., and Geis, G. (1983). "White Collar Crime Seriousness: Assessment of Police Chiefs and Regulatory Agencies Investigators." *American Journal of Police*, 3, 1–16.

Poortinga, E., Lemmen, C., and Jibson, M. D. (2006). "A Case Control Study: White Collar Defendants Compared to Defendants Charged with Nonviolent Theft." *Journal of the American Academy of Psychiatry and Law*, 34, 82–89.

PwC/Pricewaterhousecoopers (2007). *Economic Crime: People, Culture, and Controls*. The 4th Biennial Global Economic Crime Survey. United States of America, PricewaterhouseCoopers, www.pwc.com/crimesurvey., downloaded March 3, 2013.

Ragatz, L. L., Fremouw, W., and Baker, E. (2012). "The Psychological Profile of White Collar Offenders: Demographics, Criminal Thinking, Psychopathic Traits, and Psychopathology." *Criminal Justice and Behavior*, 39 (7), 978–997.

Ravn, L. K. and Schultz, J. (2011). "Tiltale sendt i retur (Prosecution returned)." *Dagens Næringsliv*, August 15, 13.

Reiss-Andersen, B. (2011). "Uakseptabel mistenkeliggjøring (Unacceptable suspicion)." *Dagens Næringsliv*, September 11, 34.

Reiss-Andersen, B. (2012). "Røverhistorie på avveie (Wrong story o nits way)." *Dagens Næringsliv*, December 4, 39.

Rendal, S. and Westerby, T. (2010). Hvilke forventninger har revisor i forhold til brukere avfinansiell informasjon når det gjelder revisors plikter til forebygging og avdekking av misligheter?,(What expectations do auditors have in relation to users of financial information when it comes to auditors' duties to prevent and detect potential crime?) Master of Science thesis, BI Norwegian Business School, Oslo..

Renå, H. (2012). *Norges integritetssystem—ikke helt perfekt? (Norwegian Integrity System – Not quite perfect?)* Oslo: Transparency International Norge.

Robb, G. (2006). "Women and White-Collar Crime." *British Journal of Criminology*, 46, 1058–1072.

Rosenmerkel, S. P. (2001). "Wrongfulness and Harmfulness as Components of Serious White Collar Offenders." *Journal of Contemporary Criminal Justice*, 17, 308–327.

Samociuk, M. and Iyer, N. (2009). *A Short Guide to Fraud Risk*. UK: Gower Publishing.

Schnatterly, K. (2003). "Increasing Firm Value through Detection and Prevention of White-Collar Crime." *Strategic Management Journal*, 24 (7), 587–614.

Shanzenbach, M. and Yaeger, M. (2006). "Prison Time, Fines, and Federal White Collar Criminals: The Anatomy of a Racial Disparity." *Journal of Criminal Law Criminology*, 96, 757–793.

Sheptycki, J. (2007). "Police Ethnography in the House of Serious and Organized Crime," in Henry, A. and Smith, D. J. (editors), *Transformations of Policing*. Oxford, UK: Ashgate Publishing, 51–77.

Silverstone, H. and Sheetz, M. (2003). *Forensic Accounting and Fraud Investigation for Non-Experts*. Hoboken, N. J.: J. Wiley & Sons, Inc..

Simpson, S. S. (2011). "Making Sense of White Collar Crime: Theory and Research." *The Ohio State Journal of Criminal Law*, 8 (2), 481–502.

Simpson, S. S. and Weisburd, D., editors (2009). *The Criminology of White-Collar Crime*. New York: Springer.

Søreide, T. (2006). Business Corruption: Incidents, Mechanisms, and Consequences. Thesis submitted for PhD, Norwegian School of Economics and Business Administration, Bergen, Norway.

Stadler, W. A. and Benson, M. L. (2012). "Revisiting the Guilty Mind: The Neutralization of White-Collar Crime." *Criminal Justice Review*, 37 (4), 494–511.

Stadler, W. A., Benson, M. L., and Cullen, F. T. (2013). "Revisiting the Special Sensitivity Hypothesis: The Prison Experience of White-Collar Inmates." *Justice Quarterly*, iFirst, 1–25.

Susskind, R. (2010). *The End of Lawyers? Rethinking the Nature of Legal Services*. Oxford: Oxford University Press.

Sutherland, E. H. (1940). "White Collar Criminality." *American Sociological Review*, 5, 1–12.

Sutherland, E. H. (1949). *White Collar Crime*. New York: Holt Rinehart and Winston.

Sutherland, E. H. (1983). *White Collar Crime: The Uncut Version*. New Haven, CT: Yale University Press.

Sutton, R. I. and Staw, B. M. (1995). "What Theory Is Not." *Administrative Science Quarterly*, 40, 371–384.

Sykes, G. and Matza, D. (1957). "Techniques of Neutralization: A Theory of Delinquency." *American Sociological Review*, 22 (6), 664–670.

Søreide, T. (2006). *Business corruption: Incidence, mechanisms, and consequences*. Thesis submitted for the PhD at the Norwegian School of Economics and Business Administration, Bergen, Norway.

Tombs, S. and Whyte, D. (2007). *Safety Crimes*. Oregon: Willan Publishing.

Trautner, M. (2011). "Tort Reform and Access to Justice: How Legal Environments Shape Lawyers' Case Selection." *Qualitative Sociology*, 34 (4), 523–538.

Trustpilot (2013). "Egeparken anmeldelser (Egeparken complaints)." Trustpilot, downloaded January 3, 2013, http://www.trustpilot.dk/review/www.egeparken.dk

Vanvik, H. (2011). "Diamantring fra skatteparadis (Diamond Ring from Tax Haven)." *Dagens Næringsliv*, February 3, 4–5.
Wagner, R. E. (2011). "Gordon Gekko to the Rescue? Insider Trading as a Tool to Combat Accounting Fraud,." *University of Cincinnati Law Review*, 79, 973–993.
Wang, W. T. (2009). "Knowledge Management Adoption in Times of Crisis." *Industrial Management & Data Systems*, 109 (4), 445–462.
Vanvik, H. (2010). "Har vært en heksejakt (Has been a witch hunt)." *Dagens Næringsliv*, October 13, 14.
Warhuus, C. (2011). *Present principle: The role of auditing in detection of white-collar crime*, Master of Science thesis, BI Norwegian Business School, Oslo, Norway.
Walters, G. D. and Geyer, M. D. (2004). "Criminal Thinking and Identity in Male White Collar Offenders." *Criminal Justice and Behavior*, 31, 263–281.
Weber, R. (2003). "Theoretically Speaking, Editor's Comments." *MIS Quarterly*, 27 (3), iii–xii.
Weisburd, D., Wheeler, S., Waring, E., and Bode, N. (1991). *Crimes of the Middle Classes*, New Haven, CT: Yale University Press.
Wheeler, S. (1992). "The Problem of White Collar Crime Motivation," in *White Collar Crime Reconsidered*, Schlegel, K. and Weisburd, D. (editors), Boston: Northeastern University Press, 108–123.
Wheeler, S., Mann, K. and Sarat, A. (1988). *Sitting in the Judgment. The Sentencing of White Collar Offenders.* New Haven, CT: Yale University Press.
Wheeler, S., Weisburd, D. and Bode, N. (1982). "Sentencing the White Collar Offender. Rhetoric and Reality." *American Sociological Review*, 47, 641–656.
Wheeler, S., Weisburd, D., Waring, E., and Bode, N. (1988). "White Collar Crimes and Criminals." *American Criminal Law Review*, 25, 331–357.
Williams, K. M. and Paulhus, D. I. (2004). "Factor Structure of the Self-Report Psychopathy Scale (SRP-II) in Non-Forensic Samples." *Personality and Individual Differences*, 37, 765–778.
Wright, A. (2006). *Organised Crime*. Devon, UK: Willan Publishing.
Zack, M. H. (1999). "Developing a Knowledge Strategy." *California Management Review*, 41 (3), 125–145.
Ånestad, M. (2013). "Vil kjempe for ny sak (Will fight for a new trial)." *Dagens Næringsliv*, May 4, 9.

Index

acceptable mistake, 129
age of criminal, 141
age of lawyer, 141
agency theory, 124–126
Andenæs, Ellen Holager, 35, 149
appeal to higher loyalties, 128
attorney-client asymmetry, 53–54
attorney-client privilege, 61–64, 144
attribution theory, 129–130
auditing role, 31–34

Brosveet, Anders, 149, 150

claim to entitlement, 128
condemnation of condemners, 128
conflict of interest, 125
conspiracy theory, 130–131
core competence, 90–92
corporate crime, 20, 138, 173, 174
corruption, 17, 22, 28–30
court, 173–180
criminal organization, 125, 126

defense attorney, 61, 65
defense lawyer, 68, 70
defense lawyer strategies, 55
denial of injury, 128
denial of responsibility, 128
denial of victim, 128
dilemma tradeoff, 129

Elden, John Christian, 61, 159, 160
explicit knowledge, 80

financial crime, 22
first-time offender, 144–147
fraud, 21–25

Hermansen, Robert, 34

illegal monopoly, 125
income of criminal, 141
income of lawyer, 141, 150
information control, 60–64, 165
information sources, 64–69, 165
involved persons, 153, 165

judge, 173

Keiserud, Erik, 149, 150
know-how, 45, 177
knowledge management, 84
knowledge organization, 86, 87, 93–101
knowledge rivalry, 177
knowledge sharing, 97, 98
knowledge worker, 110, 112, 119
know-what, 45, 177
know-why, 45, 177

law firm, 93–106
lawyer clients, 44, 45, 49
lawyer fame, 142
lawyer income, 141, 150
learning organization, 101–103
legal mistake, 128
Lyngtveit, Erling, 149, 150

manipulation, 22, 26–28
media, 60, 73
money in crime, 158

neutralization theory, 127–129
normality of action, 128

occupational crime, 13, 20

police investigation, 59, 60, 72
policing strategies, 50, 73
prison sentence, 142, 158
prosecutor, 173

Reiss-Andersen, Berit, 149, 150
resource-based theory, 94, 117–118
Røkke, Kjell Inge, 35

stages of growth theory, 131–133
Stordrange, Bjørn, 58, 72, 75, 147, 150
substance defense, 56–59, 165
symbolic defense, 72–75, 165

tacit knowledge, 80
theft, 22, 25–26
transaction cost, 119–122
Transocean, 50–53

value shop, 103–104

white-collar crime, 13–18
white-collar criminal, 18–21

Printed in the United States of America